# CHAIN MAIL PLUS

## Jewelry Projects Using Crystals, Charms & More

### SANDY HAUGEN

KALMBACH BOOKS

Waukesha, Wisconsin

**Kalmbach Books**
21027 Crossroads Circle
Waukesha, Wisconsin 53186
www.JewelryAndBeadingStore.com

Published in 2018
22 21 20 19 18    1 2 3 4 5

Manufactured in China

ISBN: 978-1-62700-385-8
EISBN: 978-1-62700-386-5


**Editor:** Erica Barse
**Book Design:** Lisa Schroeder
**Photographer:** William Zuback


**Library of Congress Control Number:** 2016943723

# CONTENTS

# INTRODUCTION

When I was explaining to someone several months ago that I was writing a book about making chain mail jewelry, she was surprised. She had no idea that chain mail could be used in jewelry. For her, as for many people, chain mail meant the armor that was worn by knights in medieval Europe.

And they're right. Chain mail (which is a series of small metal rings linked together in a pattern) was used to create protective body armor in Europe in the Middle Ages. However, this is only one piece of a much larger picture. Chain mail existed even before the Middle Ages, with examples of chain mail made by the Etruscans (in what is now Italy) dating back to about 400 B.C. It was also used in many countries throughout Europe, Asia, North Africa and the Middle East, and was used by many cultures including the ancient Egyptians and the Vikings. Chain mail as armor continues to be used today in butcher's gloves, in shark-resistant diving suits, and by groups dedicated to the re-creation and re-enactment of Medieval European cultures.

In addition to being used in armor, in some ancient cultures, chain mail was used for decorative purposes, such as jewelry. Today, there are literally hundreds of ornamental chain mail weaves and they are used to create an astonishing diversity of items: jewelry, sculpture, clothing, banners and wall hangings, baskets and containers, purses and wallets, neckties and scarves, and more.

Chain mail jewelry is beautiful all on its own, with intricate weaves and patterns created in metals such as gold, silver, and copper. However, one of the things I love about chain mail is that you can also embellish it in so many ways to take your jewelry piece beyond the traditional chain mail weave. You can use colored rings in your weave and you can add a huge variety of other elements to it: beads (such as crystals, Czech glass, gemstones, and pearls), metal components (such as charms, links, buttons, and chain), leather (such as flat, round, or bolo cord), other cords (such as rattail satin, paracord, and kumihimo braided cord), and ribbon (such as satin and silk). I think of this as chain mail *plus*, and that's what I'll be sharing with you in this book.

## HOW TO USE THIS BOOK

- The projects are arranged by jewelry type: earrings are first, followed by bracelets, then necklaces, and finally by jewelry sets. You will learn different chain mail weaves along the way while you are making these pieces of jewelry.

- All the chain mail instructions you need are included within each project. This means that you don't need to complete the projects in any particular order. You can start with the first project, the last one, or any one you wish.

- All measurements in the book are given in both Imperial (inches, feet) and metric (mm, cm). Each project includes the finished sizes for the earring, bracelet, and/or necklace.

- Each project has detailed info about the jump rings, including number of rings used, how many need to be opened/closed, AWG, ID, and AR. All wire gauges for the projects are AWG.

- The acronyms in the point above are explained in the Chain Mail Techniques and Tips section at the end of the book. This section also includes information about holding your pliers and jump rings, opening and closing rings, and other useful tips.

Project instructions are written from my perspective as a right-handed person. If you are left-handed, you'll need to reverse them.

And one last point …

At the end of each project, I've included a section with alternate design ideas and suggestions for different component options that will allow you to personalize the jewelry to suit your style. My hope is that it will encourage you to imagine other possibilities for the weave and may inspire you to create some original chain mail *plus* of your own.

Happy mailling!

— Sandy

# TOOLS

## PLIERS

Two pairs of jewelry pliers (one to be held in each hand) are the cornerstone for making chain mail. These can be flatnose, chainnose, or bent chainnose pliers, or any combination of these. When I'm working on a weave, my preference is to have chainnose pliers in my right (dominant) hand and bent chainnose pliers in my left hand. I find that this combination works well for me in maneuvering into some of the tighter spaces within a weave. When I'm opening and closing a large batch of jump rings for mailling, I will sometimes switch to flatnose pliers instead. Try different combinations to find what works best for you.

Your pliers don't need to be expensive, although there's certainly nothing wrong with investing in higher-end pliers if you wish. My current favorites are a pair of fine-nosed pliers with shorter, ergonomic handles, which fit nicely in my hands and were less than $10 each.

It's essential that your pliers have smooth (not serrated) jaws so they don't mark your jump rings. You can also use a file or sandpaper to smooth any sharp edges. Look for pliers with a good joint and with a spring that keeps the jaws open when not in use.

You will also need some basic wire-working jewelry tools—roundnose pliers and wire-cutting pliers (side cutters and/or flush cutters)—in order to attach beads to your chain mail.

Side cutters

Flush cutters

Flatnose pliers

Roundnose pliers

Chainnose pliers

Bent chainnose pliers

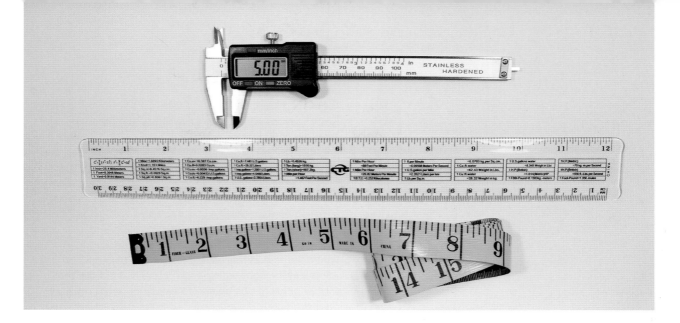

## MEASURING TOOLS

A straight ruler and a flexible tape measure are useful for measuring many items, such as the length of the chain you are weaving, the size of a wrist for a bracelet, or the length of ribbon or leather you are attaching to your chain mail. Digital calipers are useful if you need to measure the inside diameter (ID) or outside diameter (OD) of your jump rings.

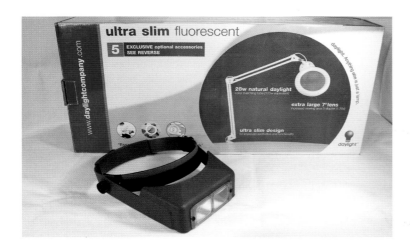

## LIGHTING AND MAGNIFICATION

In order to create chain mail that looks well-made and professional, you need to be able to clearly see what you are doing. Good daylight-spectrum lighting is important. Consider where you do your mailling and whether or not the lighting needs to be movable. Track lighting in a craft studio, a floor lamp beside your kitchen table, or a portable task light can all be reasonable solutions.

Magnification is also important in order to see whether the ends of your rings are closed properly. Again, consider how portable this needs to be for you. Desktop or clamp-on magnifiers, headband magnifiers, and eyeglass magnifiers are some of the available options.

There are also solutions that combine both lighting and magnification, in desktop and clamp-on versions and in LED lighting that attaches to headband magnifiers.

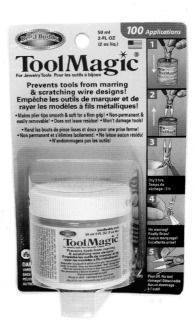

## TOOL MAGIC

Tool Magic is a rubbery coating designed for jewelry tools. It can prevent your pliers from scratching the finish off of your jump rings. It also helps you hold onto your rings more easily, without having them slip out of your grip. Simply open the lid of the jar, stir with a toothpick, and dip the tips of your pliers into the liquid. Let them dry for a few hours, with the tips either upright or hanging over an edge so nothing is touching them, and then they're ready to use. The coating will eventually show some "wear and tear." When it does, just peel it off, wipe down your pliers with a damp cloth, and apply a fresh coat.

## CHAIN MAIL MAT

Beading mats sometimes have fibers that jump rings can catch on. What I have found that works well for chain mail are 9"x12" (23x30cm) craft foam sheets. I usually end up buying the 12"x18" (30x46cm) sheets and cutting them in half. I find that the slight "give" of their surface allows me to get my pliers underneath the edge of a closed ring to pick it up more easily. I tend to use a mat color that contrasts with the jump rings I am mailling. A dark-colored mat makes it easier to see light-colored rings, and a light-colored mat makes it easier to see dark-colored rings. I find that the contrasting background color of the mat further helps me be able to tell whether or not my jump rings are tightly closed.

## CUTTING TOOLS

You will need a strong, sharp pair of scissors for cutting leather and other cord to attach to your chain mail. A smaller pair of scissors is helpful for cutting ribbon and thread. A sturdy utility knife is useful for cutting mats and trimming any ragged edges of leather and other cord.

## OTHER TOOLS

Twist ties, when attached to your chain mail, provide a "handle" to hang onto when you are starting a weave. They are sometimes also required to provide stability for a weave; in other words, to prevent pieces from coming undone until you have finished them, such as by attaching a clasp to the ends or inserting a cord through the weave. Also, if it's important to be able to identify which is the starting point of your weave and which is the end point, you can use different colors of twist ties at each end. Just make sure to remember (or write down) which one is the start color and which one is the end color! You can also use pieces of craft wire instead of twist ties.

You can use toothpicks to help identify and open the pathway where you need to insert your jump ring. They can often hold the pathway open until you have passed the ring through it. They can also be used to clean excess glue from around the edges of a glued-on clasp.

Hand-sewing needles and straight pins are necessary when you are attaching ribbon to your chain mail.

## JUMP RINGS

Jump rings are available in a wide variety of metals, including aluminum, brass, bronze, copper, silver, gold, niobium, titanium, steel, and other metals. Each metal has different properties of weight, hardness, and springback (the tendency of metal to return to its original shape after it has been bent). Jump rings are most commonly made with round wire, but can also be made with half-round, square, or twisted wire. Jump rings are typically round, but can also be oval, triangular, or square.

To make jump rings, the wire is wrapped around a mandrel to produce coils, which are then cut into individual rings. There are different methods of cutting the coils, including pinch cutting (cut with side cutter pliers), machine cutting (cut using shearing action), and saw cutting (cut with a rotary blade or jeweler's saw). Pinch cut and machine cut rings have irregular ends, which cannot be closed to a tight join. Saw cut rings are the best type for jewelry, as they can be closed to a nearly seamless join.

The majority of the projects in this book are made with anodized aluminum jump rings. Anodizing is a process involving chemicals and electricity, resulting in a colored coating on the rings. Niobium and titanium rings are also anodized for color. Because of the complexity of the process, the colors can vary a bit from one batch to another, so it is best to ensure you buy enough rings at one time to complete your project.

Anodized aluminum jump rings are lightweight, inexpensive, and come in many colors, sizes, and wire gauges. They are stronger than copper rings, but not as hard as steel or titanium. They do not tarnish, so the bright silver anodized rings retain their shiny color.

Several projects in this book are made with TierraCast jump rings. These are available in four different sizes and gauges of round jump rings, as well as two sizes of oval jump rings. The rings come in six different finishes (including silver, gold, copper, and black) which match the finishes of other TierraCast jewelry components. These jump rings are made with plated brass or solid copper, so they are heavier than the comparable size in anodized aluminum. They are also less hard and have less springback than anodized aluminum, which makes them a bit easier to close tightly.

Silver-plated and copper rings will tarnish over time if not protected, as does everything that is made with these metals. Anti-tarnish strips and jewelry bags can prevent tarnishing, and a jeweler's polishing cloth can be used to remove tarnish.

# MATERIALS

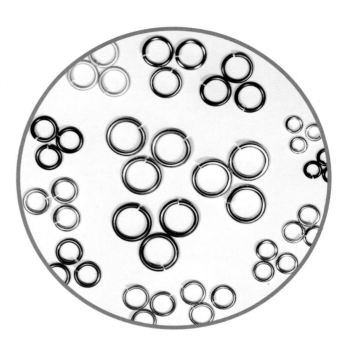

## JUMP RINGS

| Material | Inside Diameter (ID) | Wire Gauge | Aspect Ratio (AR) |
|---|---|---|---|
| ANODIZED ALUMINUM | 2.4MM (3/32") | 20 AWG | 3.0 |
| ANODIZED ALUMINUM | 3.4MM (1/8") | 20 AWG | 4.2 |
| ANODIZED ALUMINUM | 4.3MM (5/32") | 20 AWG | 5.3 |
| ANODIZED ALUMINUM | 4.1MM (5/32") | 18 AWG | 4.1 |
| ANODIZED ALUMINUM | 5.0MM (3/16") | 18 AWG | 5.0 |
| ANODIZED ALUMINUM | 6.7MM (1/4") | 16 AWG | 5.5 |
| PLATED BRASS | 4MM (.149") | 20 AWG | 4.7 |
| PLATED BRASS | 5MM (.195") | 16 AWG | 3.8 |
| PLATED BRASS | 6MM (.215") | 19 AWG | 6.0 |
| COPPER | 3.25MM (1/8") | 22 AWG | 5.1 |
| COPPER | 2.11 X 3.18 MM (.083 X .125") | 20 AWG | Not applicable for oval rings |

**Swarovski
crystals**

**TierraCast
charms**

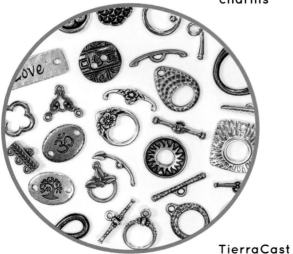

**TierraCast
clasps and links**

## SWAROVSKI CRYSTALS

Swarovski is an Austrian-based company that produces crystal figurines, jewelry, and jewelry components. Swarovski crystal is world-renowned for its beauty, precision, and quality. There are a multitude of Swarovski crystal beads, pendants, and other elements that can be added to chain mail. Their pendants can often be added by passing a jump ring directly through the hole in the crystal. Beads can be added by inserting a headpin through the bead, making a wrapped loop at the other end, and passing a jump ring through the wrapped loop. You will see crystals adorning many of the projects in this book.

## TIERRACAST COMPONENTS

TierraCast is a company based in Santa Rosa, California, that designs and manufactures lead-free pewter jewelry components. They produce a wide variety of jewelry-making products, including beads, buttons, caps, cones, bails, charms, pendants, links, clasps, chain, and leather findings. TierraCast components are plated with a range of finishes, including bright silver, antiqued silver, bright rhodium, bright gold, antiqued gold, antiqued copper, black, and brass oxide; these finishes match across their product lines. Their finely-detailed and consistently high-quality products make TierraCast one of my favorite suppliers, and I have used them for many projects in this book.

## OTHER BEADS AND PENDANTS

There are so many other types of beads and pendants you can add to your chain mail that it's not possible to list them all. You may use:

- Czech glass (such as fire-polished, pressed glass, and lampworked beads)
- Precious gemstones (such as emerald, ruby, sapphire, and diamond)
- Semiprecious gemstones (such as turquoise, amethyst, and jade)
- Pearls (such as natural, cultured, freshwater, and glass or crystal pearls)
- Shells (such as paua/abalone and mother-of-pearl)
- Ceramic and porcelain

## HEADPINS, EYEPINS, AND EARRING WIRES

Headpins and eyepins are used to attach beads to your chain mail, and earwires are used in making earrings. These items are available from several manufacturers and you may already have one or more favorites among these.

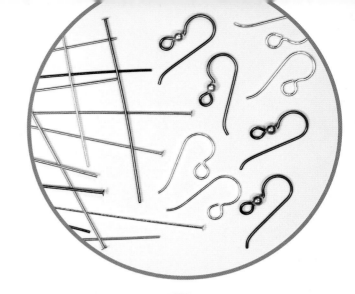

I generally use 21-gauge 2" headpins and eyepins. For beads with small holes, I usually use 24-gauge 2" headpins and eyepins in copper, sterling silver, and gold-filled.

For my earring projects, choose from earring wires in sterling silver, gold-filled, or niobium (with black or copper finish). Earring wires come in several shapes and can be plain or have beads and/or coils above the loop. A TierraCast regular loop earring wire has a loop that is large enough to contain several jump rings, so I can place an entire chain mail flower link within the loop.

## CORD, RIBBON, AND CHAIN

Leather and faux-leather cord can be added to chain mail by a number of methods, such as threading it through jump rings, wrapping a weave around it, or using it to join two pieces of a weave together. You can use round leather, flat leather, or bolo cord in a variety of sizes, depending on your chain mail design. Other types of cord that can be used include rattail satin cord, paracord, and kumihimo braided cord. Satin ribbon, silk ribbon, and other types of ribbon can also be woven through a chain mail weave. Chain can be used to join two pieces of a chain mail weave or to attach dangling embellishments to earrings or other jewelry pieces.

## OTHER MATERIALS

E6000 is my favorite glue for jewelry, particularly for attaching end caps and glue-on clasps. It's extremely strong, it dries clear, and it doesn't bond to skin (like some of the "instant" glues do). It's important to follow the manufacturer's instructions, which include making sure to allow enough time (24–72 hours) for the glue to cure and to use it in a well-ventilated area.

For projects in this book that have ribbon woven through the chain mail, sewing thread is used in attaching and finishing the ribbon ends. I find that polyester thread works well for this, but you could use nylon thread as well.

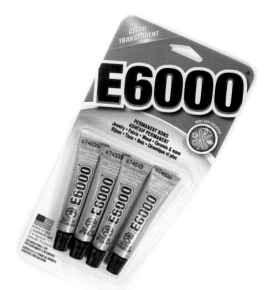

5.3 mL

# EARRINGS

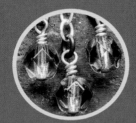  

# TRENDING TRIANGLES

In these earrings, a modified Japanese 12-in-2 weave forms a triangle chandelier, which becomes the base for chain-and-bead dangles. This is a versatile design you can modify in many ways, from making basic earrings for everyday wear to creating an elegant fashion statement.

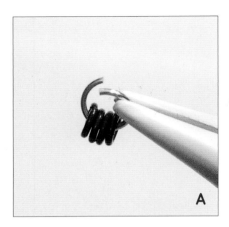

A

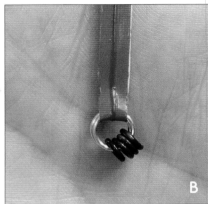

B

C

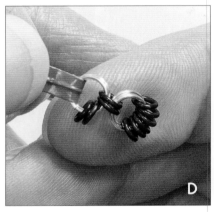

D

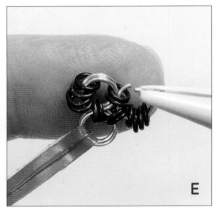

E

## MATERIALS >>

*Earring size: 2¼" (5.7cm)*

- Anodized aluminum jump rings
  - » **24** 20-gauge ⁵/₃₂" (4.3mm) ID, bright silver [AR 5.3]
  - » **48** 20-gauge ³/₃₂" (2.4mm) ID, purple [AR 3.0]
- **6** 21-gauge or 22-gauge 1½" (3.8cm) headpins, sterling silver or rhodium plated
- **6** 6mm lilac/mint fire-polished Czech glass faceted round beads
- 5" (13cm) 24-gauge 4x3mm oval cable chain, sterling silver or rhodium plated
- Pair of sterling silver earring wires

## TOOLS >>

- **2** pairs of pliers (chainnose, bent chainnose, and/or flatnose)
- Twist ties
- Roundnose pliers
- Side cutters
- Ruler or tape measure

## MAKE THE TRIANGLE CHANDELIER

**1|** Close 18 purple jump rings and open 12 silver jump rings **(Chain Mail Techniques and Tips, p. 104)**. Pick up an open silver ring and use it to pick up four closed purple rings **[A]**.

**2|** Close the silver ring. Add another open silver ring beside it, following the same path, and close the ring. Place a twist tie through the two silver rings. This will be the "handle" to help you hold and stabilize the weave **[B]**.

**3|** Pick up an open silver ring and use it to pick up six closed purple rings; then, place it through the two right-hand purple rings attached to the first set of silver rings **[C]**.

**4|** Close the silver ring. Add another open silver ring beside it, following the same path (through all eight purple rings), and close the ring **[D]**.

**5|** Pick up an open silver ring and use it to pick up four closed purple rings. Pass it through the two left-hand purple rings in the first set of silver rings plus the two left-hand purple rings in the second set of silver rings **[E]**.

F

G

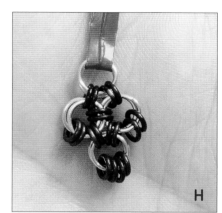

H

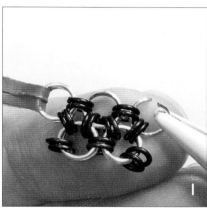

I

J

K

**6|** Close the silver ring. Add another open silver ring beside it, following the same path, and close the ring. You will now have a small triangle, and the sets of silver rings in the bottom row will each have four "loose" purple rings in them **[F]**.

**7|** Pick up an open silver ring and use it to pick up four closed purple rings. Pass it through the two right-hand purple rings in the left set of silver rings and through the two left-hand purple rings in the right set of silver rings **[G]**.

**8|** Close the silver ring. Add another open silver ring beside it, following the same path, and close the ring. You will now have a small diamond shape. There will be two "loose" purple rings in both the left and right middle sets of silver rings, and four "loose" purple rings in the bottom set of silver rings **[H]**.

**9|** Pick up an open silver ring and pass it through the two right-hand purple rings in the bottom set of silver rings and through the two remaining "loose" purple rings in the middle right set of silver rings. Close the silver ring. Add another open silver ring beside it, following the same path, and close the ring **[I]**.

**10|** Pick up an open silver ring and pass it through the two remaining sets of "loose" purple rings **[J]**.

**11|** Close the silver ring. Add another open silver ring beside it, following the same path, and close the ring. You have now completed the triangle chandelier **[K]**.

L

M

N

O

P

**5|** Repeat steps 3 and 4 to attach the ¾" pieces of chain and fire-polished beads to the left and right sets of silver jump rings on the bottom of the triangle chandelier **[O]**.

**6|** Remove the twist tie from the top of your triangle chandelier. Open the bottom loop of an earring wire, as you would a jump ring. Place the set of silver rings at the top of the triangle chandelier inside the open ear wire loop **[P]**. Close the loop.

**7|** Repeat to make a second earring.

## MAKE CHAIN-AND-BEAD DANGLES

**1|** Cut three pieces of chain with the side cutters: one piece 1" (2.54cm) and two pieces ¾" (1.9cm) long. Open six purple jump rings.

**2|** String a fire-polished bead on a headpin and make a wrapped loop at the other end **(Basic Jewelry Techniques, p. 110) [L]**. Repeat this step twice for a total of three fire-polished beads with wrapped loops.

**3|** Pick up an open purple ring and connect the wrapped loop on a fire-polished bead and the last link at one end of the 1" chain. Close the ring **[M]**.

**4|** Pick up an open purple ring and connect the last link at the other end of the 1" chain and the middle set of silver rings on the bottom of the triangle chandelier. Close the ring **[N]**.

## Design Variations

- Vary the chain lengths, either longer or shorter, for the beaded dangles.

- Use a different type of chain: Try curb or figaro chain.

- Change the bead for the dangle: Try crystal bicones or briolettes.

# TIMELESS TRISKELE

The triskele (or triskelion) is an ancient Celtic symbol that has three interlocking spirals arising from a central point. There are several interpretations of the symbol's meaning, including Father-Son-Holy Spirit, past-present-future, life-death-rebirth, and spirit-mind-body. In these earrings, the spiraling swirls of chain-mail flower links echo and enhance the triskele design.

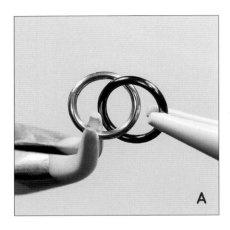

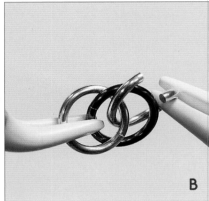

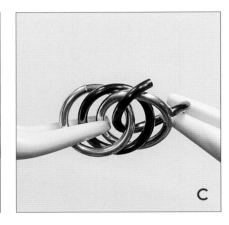

## MATERIALS >>

*Earring size: 2¾" (7cm)*

- Anodized aluminum jump rings

  » **4** 16-gauge ¼" (6.7mm) ID, bright silver [AR 5.5]

  » **4** 16-gauge ¼" (6.7mm) ID, red [AR 5.5]

  » **8** 18-gauge 3/16" (5.0mm) ID, bright silver [AR 5.0]

  » **8** 18-gauge 3/16" (5.0mm) ID, red [AR 5.0]

  » **18** 18-gauge 5/32" (4.1mm) ID, bright silver [AR 4.1]

  » **8** 18-gauge 5/32" (4.1mm) ID, red [AR 4.1]

- **2** small Triskele charms, TierraCast, antique silver

- Pair of Regular Loop earring wires, TierraCast, sterling silver

*NOTE: The bottom loop of TierraCast regular earring wires are large enough to hold the flower link. Other earring wires may not be large enough to fit the link.*

## TOOLS >>

- **2** pairs of pliers (chainnose, bent chainnose, and/or flatnose)
- Toothpicks

## MAKE THE EARRINGS

**1|** For each earring, you will use two ¼" bright silver jump rings (which we'll call the "large silver rings"), four 3/16" bright silver jump rings (which we'll call the "medium silver rings"), and nine 5/32" bright silver jump rings (which we'll call the "small silver rings.") Close one large silver ring, two medium silver rings, and two small silver rings (**Chain Mail Techniques and Tips, p. 104**). Open the rest of the silver rings.

You will also use two ¼" red jump rings (which we'll call the "large red rings"), four 3/16" red rings (which we'll call the "medium red rings"), and four 5/32" red jump rings (which we'll call the "small red rings"). Open all the red rings.

**2|** Pick up an open large red ring and use it to pick up the closed large silver ring. Close the large red ring. Position the rings so they overlap to create an "eye." Make sure the large red ring lies on top of the large silver ring on the upper side of the eye (and it will also lie underneath the large silver ring on the lower side of the eye) **[A]**.

**3|** Pick up an open large silver ring and place it through the eye you created with the previous two rings **[B]**. Close the ring.

**4|** Position the rings so each ring lies on top of the ring to its left on the upper side of the eye. Pick up an open large red ring and place it through the eye in the center of the previous three rings **[C]**. Close the ring.

**5|** You have now created a four-ring flower link **[D]**. Each ring in the link should lie on top of the ring to its left on the upper side of the eye. Move or flip the rings if necessary to get them into this position. Because each newly-added ring lies on top of the previous rings on the upper side and you flip rings up to get them into this position, we are going to call this formation an "up-link."

**6|** Pick up an open medium red ring and use it to pick up a closed medium silver ring. Close the medium red ring. Position the rings so they overlap to create an "eye." This time, make sure the medium red ring lies on top of the medium silver ring on the lower side of the eye (it will also lie underneath the medium silver ring on the upper side of the eye) **[E]**.

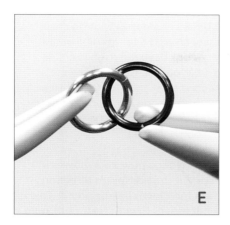

E

F

G

H

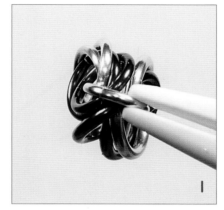

I

J

K

**7|** Pick up an open medium silver ring and place it through the eye you created with the previous two rings. Close the ring. Position the rings so each ring lies under the ring to its left on the upper side of the eye **[F]**.

**8|** Pick up an open medium red ring and place it through the eye in the center of the previous three rings **[G]**. Close the ring.

**9|** Each ring in this new flower link should lie on top of the ring to its left on the lower side of the eye. Move or flip the rings if necessary to get them into this position. Because each newly-added ring lies on top of the previous rings on the lower side and you flip rings down to get them into this position, we are going to call this formation a "down-link." Set the medium down-link next to the large up-link **[H]**. Notice how they appear to "spiral" in different directions.

**10|** Pick up an open small silver ring. Pick up the medium down-link, making sure the rings don't shift out of position, and place it onto the open small silver ring. Now pick up the large up-link, again keeping the rings in alignment, and place it on the open small silver ring, alongside the medium down-link. Close the small silver ring **[I]**.

**TIP** This is a large number of rings on the open small silver ring, and you might have to gently nudge or shake them a bit to get them to settle in and fit into the space so you can close the ring. If you find you just can't get the rings to cooperate, you can use medium silver rings to connect the flower links instead of small silver rings. This will give your earrings a slightly looser appearance and a bit of a gap between the flower links, but they will still look lovely.

**11|** Set the weave down and position it with the large up-link above the medium down-link **[J]**.

**12|** Repeat steps 6–10 to create another medium down-link and attach it to the large up-link. Set the weave down, positioning it with the large up-link in the center, and a medium down-link above and below it **[K]**.

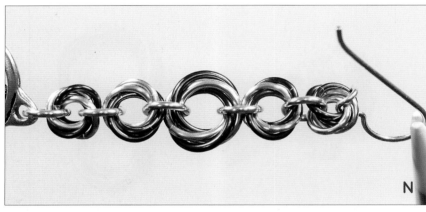

**13|** Repeat steps 2–5, using small silver and red rings in place of the large silver and red rings to create a small up-link. Repeat to create a second small up-link. Repeat step 10 to attach the small up-links to the medium down-links, one on each side of your weave **[L]**.

**TIP** Notice how each flower link "spirals" in a different direction than the flower link beside it. This is a necessary design feature to keep the earring straight. Because the weave is free-hanging, if you made the flower links all the same (either all up-links or all down-links), your earring would start to twist.

**14|** Pick up an open small silver ring. Place it through the small loop on one of the Triskele charms, then through the center of the small up-link on one end of your weave **[M]**.

**15|** Open the bottom loop of an ear wire, as you would a jump ring. Place the small up-link from the other end of your weave in the open earring wire loop, making sure you have all four rings of the flower link fully inside the loop **[N]**. Close the loop.

**16|** Repeat to make a second earring.

## Design Variations

- Try other charms or components (crystals, gemstones, etc.) in place of the Triskele charm. I prefer a flat, circular component for this design (to complement the flower links), but you can use pretty much whatever you would like to attach with a jump ring.

- Make the earrings with three flower links instead of five. Try size combinations of large-medium-small, small-medium-large, or all the same size. Whatever the combination, you must alternate up-links and down-links.

- Make the earrings without any charms or other dangles. The flower links look great on their own!

# DENIM DAYDREAMS

Copper hues of delicate queen's braid chain mail drops complement denim-blue Swarovski crystal briolette pendants in these fashionable earrings. Pair with a long denim skirt and a peasant blouse for an upscale boho-chic look.

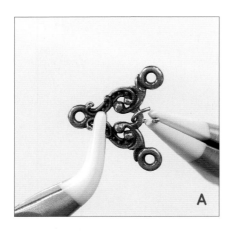

A

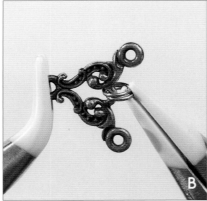

B

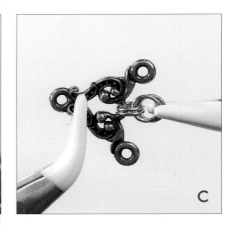

C

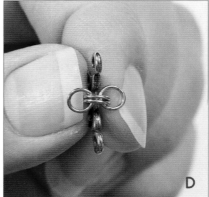

D

## MAKE THE EARRINGS

**1|** For each earring, you will use 95 copper jump rings. Open all of these rings **(Chain Mail Techniques and Tips, p. 104)**.

**2|** Pick up an open ring and place it through the center hole at the bottom of the Empire link **[A]**. Close the ring.

**3|** Add another open ring beside the first one, following the same path, and close the ring **[B]**.

**4|** Pick up an open ring and place it through the set of rings attached to the Empire link. Close the ring. Add another open ring beside it, following the same path, and close the ring **[C]**.

**5|** Grasp the weave just below the set of rings you just added. Fold back the last set of rings, one to each side, so the previous set of rings are sticking up in the middle **[D]**.

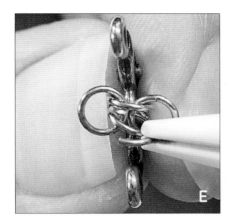

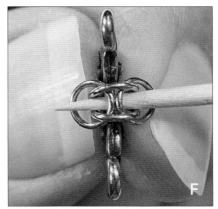

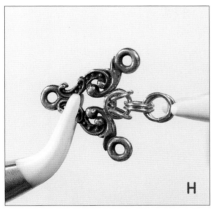

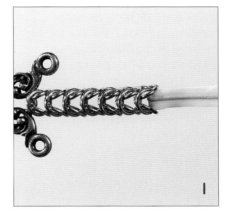

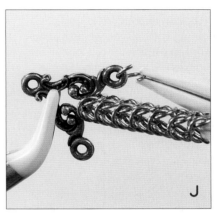

**6|** Pick up an open ring, insert it between the two rings that are sticking up in the middle, and go through the rings you folded back **[E]**. Close the ring.

TIP If you're having difficulty getting the rings in position for this step, insert a toothpick between the two rings that are sticking up in the middle and through the folded-back rings **[F]**. Use the toothpick to hold this pathway open while you insert the next ring. Once the ring is in place, remove the toothpick and close the ring.

**7|** Add another open ring beside it, following the same path, and close the ring **[G]**.

**8|** Pick up an open ring and place it through the set of rings you just added. Close the ring. Add another open ring beside it, following the same path, and close the ring **[H]**.

**9|** Repeat steps 5–8 until you have used 28 jump rings. Fold back your last set of rings and place a twist tie through them instead of a new jump ring **[I]**.

**10|** Pick up an open ring and place it through one of the side loops at the bottom of the Empire link **[J]**. Close the ring. Repeat steps 3–8 until you have used 32 jump rings. Fold back your last set of rings and place a twist tie through them instead of a new jump ring. Repeat this step on the other side loop at the bottom of the Empire link.

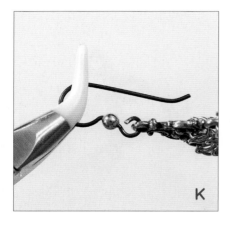

**11|** Open the bottom loop of an earring wire, as you would a jump ring, and attach the top loop of the Empire link to the earring wire **[K]**. Close the loop.

**12|** At the bottom of one of the chains attached to the Empire link, remove the twist tie and insert an open ring in its place. Also, place the ring through the hole in one of the briolette pendants **[L]**. Close the ring. Repeat this step on the other two chains attached to the Empire link.

**13|** Repeat to make a second earring.

## Design Variations

• Use different color crystals. Swarovski produces crystal briolette pendants in many colors that match well with the copper jump rings.

• Make these earrings with a variety of other beads, including other Swarovski crystal beads (such as bicones or minidrops), pearls, gemstone beads, or Czech fire-polished beads. Your maximum bead width that will fit nicely between the chain mail segments is about 6mm (1/4").

• Make the chains longer or shorter. Alter the design so the middle chain is the longest of the three, rather than the shortest. Or, alter the lengths so the outermost chain is the longest, the middle chain is shorter, and the innermost chain is the shortest (i.e. the right and left earrings will be mirror images of each other).

# BRACELETS

# CHARMS IN HARMONY

Byzantine chain mail is terrific for charm bracelets. Its stylish
structure adds distinction to the bracelet's core, and it has
symmetrical and recurring attachment points for charms on both
sides of the weave. The theme of this charm bracelet is harmony.
The gold and silver of the charms and the Byzantine segments are
placed to balance and complement each other. The charms
selected for this bracelet symbolize harmony within ourselves,
with each other, and with the earth.

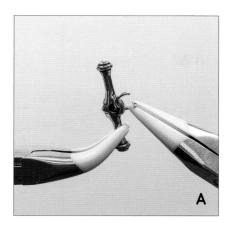

A

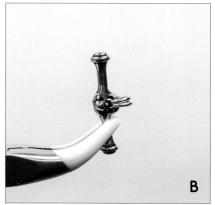

B

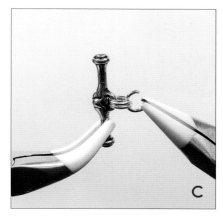

C

D

E

## MATERIALS >>

*Bracelet size: 8¼" (21cm), which fits comfortably on a 7" (17.8cm) wrist*

- Jump rings
  - » **60** 16-gauge 5mm (.195") ID, gold-plated brass [AR 3.8]
  - » **45** 16-gauge 5mm (.195") ID, silver-plated brass [AR 3.8]
  - » **8** 20-gauge 4mm (.149") ID, gold-plated brass [AR 4.7]
- **12** assorted charms, TierraCast, one each in antique gold and antique silver: Hearts, Oms, Yin Yangs, Earths, Trees, and Lotuses
- Del Sol toggle clasp, TierraCast, antique gold

## TOOLS >>

- **2** pairs of pliers (chainnose, bent chainnose, and/or flatnose)
- Toothpicks

## MAKE THE BRACELET

**1|** To create the bracelet, you will use 45 5mm silver-plated brass jump rings, 60 5mm gold-plated brass jump rings (which we'll call the "large gold rings"), and eight 4mm gold-plated brass jump rings (which we'll call the "small gold rings"). Open all of these rings **(Chain Mail Techniques and Tips, p. 104)**.

**2|** Pick up an open small gold ring and place it through the loop of the toggle bar **[A]**. Close the ring. Add another open small gold ring beside it, following the same path, and close the ring **[B]**.

**3|** Pick up an open small gold ring and place it through the previous set of rings **[C]**. Close the ring. Add another open small gold ring beside it, following the same path, and close the ring **[D]**.

F

**4|** Repeat step 3 twice for a total of four sets of small gold rings attached to the toggle bar **[E]**.

**5|** Repeat step 3 twice, this time using the large gold rings instead of the small gold rings, so you now have two sets of large gold rings attached to your chain **[F]**.

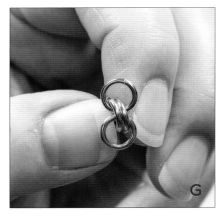

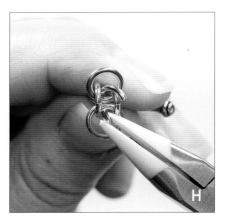

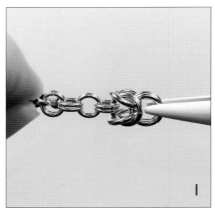

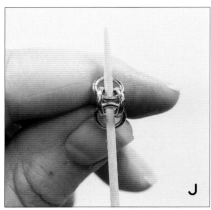

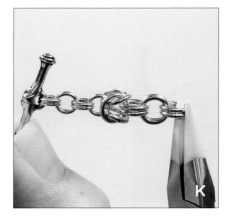

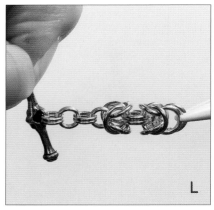

**6|** Grasp your weave just below the set of large gold rings you just added. Fold back the last set of large gold rings, one to each side, so the previous set of large gold rings is sticking up in the middle **[G]**.

**7|** Pick up an open large gold ring, insert it between the previous set of large gold rings that is sticking up in the middle, and through the large gold rings you folded back **[H]**.

**8|** Close the ring. Add another open large gold ring beside it, following the same path, and close the ring **[I]**.

**TIP** If you're having difficulty getting the rings in position for steps 6 and 7, insert a toothpick between the set of large gold rings that is sticking up in the middle and through the large gold rings you folded back **[J]**. Use the toothpick to hold this pathway open while you insert the next ring. Then, remove the toothpick and close the ring.

**9|** Follow step 3, using large gold rings instead of the small gold rings, to add two more sets of rings to the chain so you have three sets of large gold rings attached after the folded rings **[K]**.

**10|** Repeat steps 6–8, but this time attach silver rings to the folded-back large gold rings **[L]**. You have now completed a segment of Byzantine weave, which consists of two sets of folded rings facing in opposite directions, with a set of "straight" rings before them, between them, and after them.

### Byzantine at a Glance
The "formula" for Byzantine weave is pretty straightforward:
1. Join three sets of rings.
2. Perform the folding procedure.
3. Add three more sets of rings.
4. Perform the folding procedure.
5. Repeat to the desired length.

**11|** Follow steps 5–10 using silver rings to create a silver Byzantine segment. Remember the formula: add three sets of rings, fold back, add three more sets of rings, fold back again. This time, after the second fold-back, pick up a large gold ring and insert it through the folded-back rings **[M]**.

**12|** Holding onto the right side of the open large gold ring, slip the two Heart charms onto the left side of the open large gold ring in this order: first the silver charm, then the gold charm **[N]**. It doesn't matter which side of the bracelet is facing you at this point, since this step establishes which side will be the front of the bracelet. Make sure the patterned side of the charms (not the blank side) is facing toward you. Close the ring.

**TIP** In traditional Byzantine weave, you would normally place a second large gold ring beside the one just added, following the same

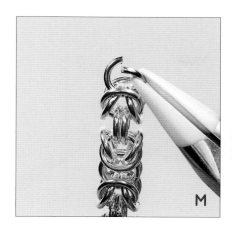
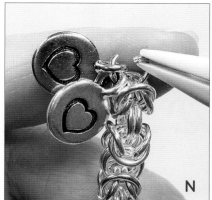

path. In this pattern, though, you are incorporating charms directly into the weave rather than adding them later by attaching them with extra jump rings—so you are not going to add the second ring. This pattern has a fairly dense weave, and adding the second ring (through the two charms and the folded-back rings) is very difficult and is not essential for the structure of the weave in this design.

**13|** Separate the charms so one lies on each side of the bracelet. Pick up an open large gold ring and insert it between the two charms **[O]**. Close the ring. Add another open large gold ring beside it, following the same path, and close the ring. This set of rings will count as the second of the three sets in your next Byzantine segment (the ring through the charms is counted as the first).

**14|** Repeat step 11 using large gold rings to create another Byzantine segment. Finish the segment by adding a silver ring after the second fold-back.

Follow step 12 to add the two Yin Yang charms onto the left side of the open silver ring in this order: first the gold charm, then the silver charm **[P]**.

Make sure the patterned side of the charms (both the Yin Yang and the Heart charms) are facing toward you. Close the ring.

**15|** Follow step 13 to separate the Yin Yang charms and place an open silver ring between them **[Q]**. Close the ring. Add another open silver ring beside it, following the same path, and close the ring. This set of rings will count as the second of the three sets in your next Byzantine segment.

**16|** Continue creating Byzantine segments and adding charms:

**a|** Add a silver Byzantine segment, finishing with a large gold ring. Add the Om charms (first the silver charm, then the gold charm), and separate them one to each side.

**b|** Add a gold Byzantine segment, finishing with a silver ring. Add the Earth charms (first the gold charm, then the silver charm), and separate them one to each side.

**c|** Add a silver Byzantine segment, finishing with a large gold ring. Add the Tree charms (first the silver charm, then the gold charm), and separate them one to each side.

**d|** Add a gold Byzantine segment, finishing with a silver ring. Add the Lotus charms (first the gold charm, then the silver charm), and separate them one to each side **[R]**.

S

T

**17|** Add a silver Byzantine segment, finishing with two large gold rings **[S]**.

**18|** Add a gold Byzantine segment and finish it with two large gold rings. Pick up an open large gold ring and place it through the last set of large gold rings **[T]**. Close the ring.

**19|** Pick up an open large gold ring and place it through the last single large gold ring. Close the ring. Pick up another open large gold ring, place it through the small hole in your toggle ring, and then through the last single large gold ring on the chain **[U]**. Close the ring.

U

## Design Variations

• Change the theme of the bracelet and choose charms to match your theme. For example: seasonal (spring flowers, autumn leaves), holidays (Halloween ghosts, Christmas bells), or special occasions (graduation caps, baby booties). You can also create a story bracelet with a selection of charms to symbolize interests, achievements, and life events.

• Place charms on a single side of the bracelet, rather than both sides.

• Make the Byzantine weave in a single color or alternate the colors for each set of rings (rather than each full Byzantine segment).

# CORD-IALLY YOURS

I love this thick, patterned cord. I was having a great time playing with pebble-print faux-leather cord, creating bracelets with beadwoven embellishments, and I decided I had to find a way to combine this cord with chain mail. After some trial and error with different jump ring sizes, I found a way to "nestle" a queen's braid weave between two pieces of the cord. The bronze rings of the chain mail contrast nicely with the turquoise cord and create an attention-getting bracelet.

- Anodized aluminum jump rings
    - » **160** 20-gauge ⁵⁄₃₂" (4.3mm) ID, bronze [AR 5.3]
    - » **28** 16-gauge ¼" (6.7mm) ID, bronze [AR 5.5]
- 15½" (39.4cm) of 6mm round stitched pebble-print faux-leather cord, turquoise
- 10.5x6.5mm (opening size) oval-shaped magnetic clasp, antique copper

- **2** pairs of pliers (chainnose, bent chainnose, and/or flatnose)
- Sharp scissors or utility knife
- Twist ties
- Toothpicks
- Facial tissues
- Ruler (or tape measure)
- E6000 glue

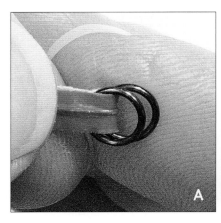

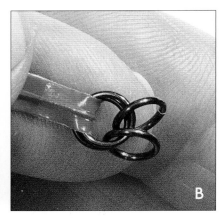

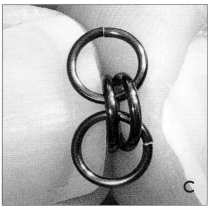

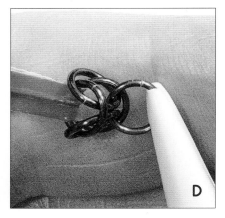

## WEAVE THE CHAIN MAIL

**1 |** You will be creating a queen's braid chain with the ⁵⁄₃₂" bronze jump rings (which we'll call the "small rings"). Close two of the small rings and open the remaining 158 small rings **(Chain Mail Techniques and Tips, p. 104)**. You will use the ¼" bronze jump rings to create the loops on the side of the weave to hold your cord. We'll call these the "large rings." Open all 28 of the large rings.

**2 |** Place a twist tie through the two closed small rings. This will be the "handle" to help you hold and stabilize the weave **[A]**.

**3 |** Pick up an open small ring and place it through the two closed rings. Close the ring. Add another open small ring beside it, following the same path, and close the ring **[B]**.

**4 |** Grasp the weave just below the set of rings you just added. Fold back the last set of rings, one to each side, so that the previous set of rings are sticking up in the middle **[C]**.

**5 |** Pick up an open small ring, and insert it between the two rings sticking up in the middle and through the rings that you folded back. Close the ring **[D]**. Add another open small ring beside it, following the same path, and close the ring.

E

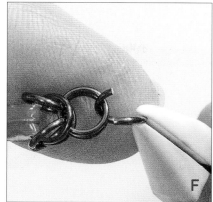

F

G

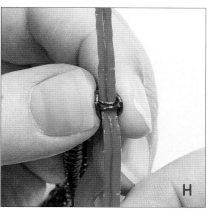

H

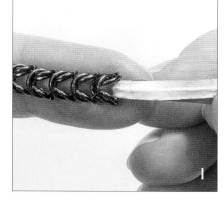

I

**TIP** If you're having difficulty getting the rings in position for this step, insert a toothpick between the two rings that are sticking up in the middle and through the folded-back rings **[E]**. Use the toothpick to hold this pathway open while you insert the next ring. Once the ring is in place, remove the toothpick and close the ring.

**6 |** Pick up an open small ring and insert it through the last set of rings added **[F]**. Close the ring. Add another open small ring beside it, following the same path, and close the ring.

**7 |** Repeat steps 4–6 until you have used all 160 of the small rings **[G]**.

**8 |** Fold back the last set of rings as in step 4. This time, insert a twist tie through the rings (instead of another open small ring as in step 5) **[H]**.

**9 |** Fold the twist tie over, to create another "handle" at the end of your weave **[I]**.

J

K

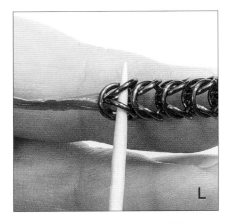

L

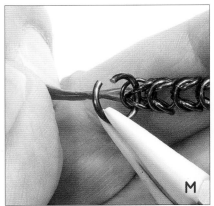

M

N

O

**10 |** You have now completed the queen's braid chain. When it is laid flat, you should see that one of the twist tie "handles" sits in a horizontal position, while the other one sits vertically **[J]**.

**TIP** You are now going to attach rings to the sides of this chain, but it is important that you leave the twist ties in place at this stage, or the ends of your weave will unfold.

**11 |** Go back to the starting point of the chain and turn the weave so the side facing you has rings aligned in a set of "V-shapes," with the point of the V facing to the left, like this: <<<<. See the V-shapes in the picture **[K]**.

**12 |** Insert a toothpick immediately behind the first left-facing V-shape **[L]**. This is the path through which you will insert your next ring.

**13 |** Pick up an open large ring and insert it through the path opened by the toothpick. Once the ring is in place, remove the toothpick and close the ring **[M]**.

**14 |** Pick up an open large ring. Skip the next two V's, and insert the ring behind the fourth V from the beginning of the chain **[N]**.

**15 |** Continue attaching large rings to every third V until you reach the end of the chain. You should end up with a large ring in the last V at the very end of the chain **[O]**. Flip the chain over, and attach a large ring to the first V, and then every third V, on the opposite side of the chain.

**16 |** You now have a queen's braid chain with large rings attached on each side. Each large ring should be attached directly opposite another large ring **[P]**.

P

Q

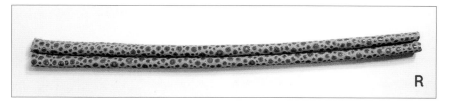

R

S

T

U

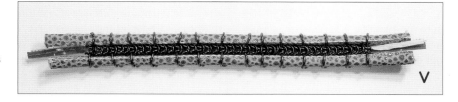

V

TIP It's important to leave the twist ties attached to the ends of your queen's braid chain. They are needed to stabilize your weave until you have placed the cord through the rings. If you remove your twist ties too soon, the ends of your weave will unfold [Q].

## ADD THE CORD

1 | Using either a pair of sharp scissors or a utility knife, cut the faux-leather cord into two 7¾" (19.7cm) pieces, making sure the ends are cut straight. It's important both pieces are the same length, or the bracelet will sit crooked on your wrist [R].

This length will provide a comfortable fit on a 7" (17.8cm) wrist. You can increase or decrease the cord length by ¼" (6.4mm), if desired.

2 | Pick up one of the pieces of cord and insert it through the first large ring on one side of the weave [S].

3 | Gently work the cord through all the large rings on that side of the weave [T].

4 | Position your cord so an approximately equal amount protrudes from the large rings at each end [U].

5 | Repeat steps 2–4 to add the second piece of cord to the other side of the weave. Line up the stitched seams of both cords so they run parallel to the top edge of the queen's braid chain [V]. Because the weave is now stabilized by the cord, you can remove the twist ties at both ends.

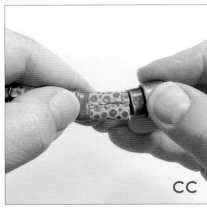

## ATTACH THE CLASP

**1 |** Squeeze the two cords together at one end of the bracelet, matching up the cord ends equally. The seams of the cord should touch **[W]**.

**2 |** Wrap a twist tie around the cords to hold them in this position **[X]**. Make sure the twist tie is far enough away from the cord ends so that it will not get glued into the clasp.

**3 |** Pick up the magnetic clasp **[Y]** and separate it into its two pieces **[Z]**.

**4 |** Squeeze a large spot of glue from the tube of E6000 onto the end of a toothpick **[AA]**. Use the toothpick to apply the glue inside one of the pieces of the magnetic clasp. Coat the bottom and sides of the clasp so it is about ⅓ to ½ full of glue **[BB]**. You might need to add a second dab of glue to accomplish this.

**5 |** Take the cord ends (that are secured by the twist tie) and push them slowly into the clasp where you have applied the glue **[CC]**. Don't let any of the cord fold back while you're inserting it and make sure the cord is pushed all the way to the bottom of the clasp. If the fit is tight, you may need to wiggle the cord a little from side to side or pinch the ends a bit with your fingers to get it into place.

**6 |** Check all around the clasp for excess glue and wipe it away with a facial tissue **[DD]**.

**7 |** If there is excess glue between the cords that is difficult to reach with a facial tissue, use a clean toothpick to remove it **[EE]**.

**8 |** Repeat steps 1–7 to attach the second piece of the clasp to the other end of the bracelet **[FF]**. Set your bracelet aside in a secure spot so the glue can properly dry and set. The manufacturer's instructions for E6000 recommend allowing 24–72 hours for the glue to cure. I wait for at least 24 hours before I pick it up and handle it, and I leave it for a minimum of 48 hours before I wear the bracelet. Once the glue has cured, you can remove the twist ties and your bracelet is completed.

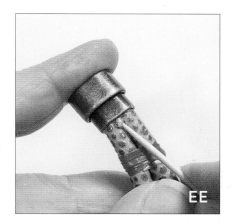

EE

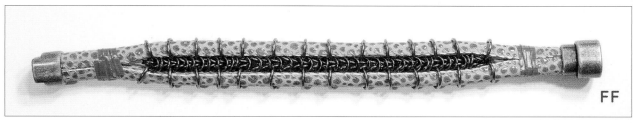

FF

## Design Variations

- You can find cord in all kinds of patterns, and you can also change the color of your pebble or snakeskin-print faux-leather cord for a bold look.

- Change the type of cord. Try other 6mm diameter cords, such as round leather, braided bolo leather, stitched suede, multi-color round cotton, or a kumihimo braid.

# AD INFINITUM

Ad Infinitum is a Latin phrase meaning "to infinity." In this bold statement bracelet, blackened infinity links are joined together by connecting segments of matte silver chain mail in a modified Byzantine weave.

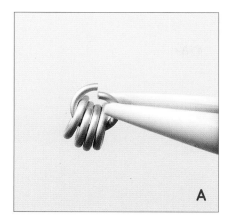 A

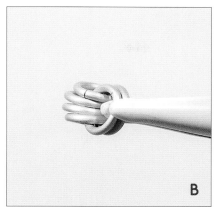 B

 C

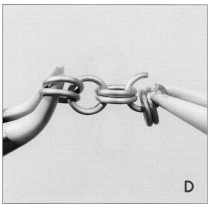 D

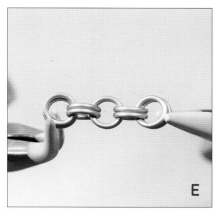 E

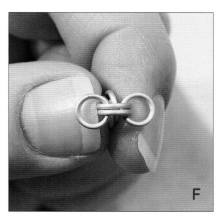 F

## MAKE THE BRACELET

**1|** You will use 180 of the 18-gauge ⁵/₃₂" matte silver rings (which we'll call the "large rings") to create the modified Byzantine chain mail segments, plus an additional six rings to attach the toggle bar. Close 60 of these rings and open 126 of them **(Chain Mail Techniques and Tips, p. 104)**.

You will use all 80 of the 20-gauge ⁵/₃₂" matte silver rings (which we'll call the "small rings") to attach the modified Byzantine segments to the Infinity links and the toggle clasp. Open all of these rings.

**2|** Pick up an open large ring and use it to pick up four closed large rings **[A]**. Close the ring.

**3|** Add another open large ring beside it, following the same path, and close the ring **[B]**.

**4|** Spread the rings out so you have a chain of three sets of two rings **[C]**.

**5|** Pick up an open large ring and use it to pick up two closed large rings. Place the open large ring through the last set of two rings on your chain **[D]**. Close the ring. Add a second ring following the same path.

**6|** Spread the rings out so you have a chain of five sets of two rings **[E]**.

**7|** Grasp the weave just below the last set of rings on one side of the chain. Fold back the last set of rings, one to each side, so the previous set of rings are sticking up in the middle **[F]**.

## MATERIALS >>

*Bracelet size: 7¾" (19.7cm), which fits comfortably on a 7" (17.8cm) wrist*

- Anodized aluminum jump rings

  » **186** 18-gauge ⁵/₃₂" (4.1mm) ID, matte silver [AR 4.1]

  » **80** 20-gauge ⁵/₃₂" (4.3mm) ID, matte silver [AR 5.3]

- **9** Infinity links, TierraCast, 32x12mm, black

- Slotted D-ring toggle clasp, TierraCast, black

## TOOLS >>

- **2** pairs of pliers (chainnose, bent chainnose, and/or flatnose)

- Toothpicks

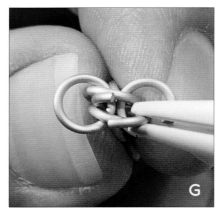

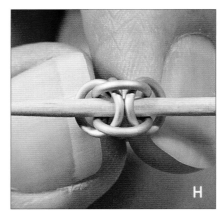

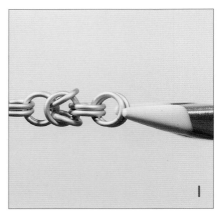

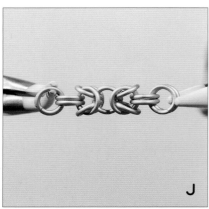

8| Pick up an open large ring, insert it between the two rings that are sticking up in the middle, and go through the rings you folded back **[G]**. Close the ring. Add another open large ring beside it, following the same path, and close the ring.

**TIP** If you're having difficulty getting the rings in position for this step, insert a toothpick between the two rings that are sticking up in the middle and through the folded-back rings **[H]**. Use the toothpick to hold this pathway open while you insert the next ring. Once the ring is in place, remove the toothpick and close the ring.

9| Pick up an open large ring and place it through the last set of rings you added. Close the ring. Add another open large ring beside it, following the same path, and close the ring. You should now have two sets of rings on your chain past the set of folded-back rings **[I]**.

10| Repeat steps 7–9 on the other side of your chain **[J]**.

11| Repeat steps 2–10 until you have a total of 10 segments. Pick up one segment and turn it so the center and end sets of rings are positioned horizontally. You should see a sideways V-shape in the set of rings to the right of the center set. You will insert your next ring behind this V-shape, through the pathway indicated by the toothpick **[K]**.

12| The Infinity links have a textured side and a smooth side. Position an Infinity link with the textured side up. Pick up an open small ring, pass it through the pathway indicated by the toothpick in the previous step, and through the upper right side of the Infinity link. Close the ring **[L]**.

M

N

O

P

Q

R

S

**13|** Farther down the same side of the chain mail segment where you inserted the small ring, you will see another sideways V-shape just on the other side of the center set of rings. You will insert your next ring behind this other V-shape, through the pathway indicated by the toothpick **[M]**.

**14|** Pick up an open small ring, pass through the pathway indicated by the toothpick in the previous step, and go through the lower right side of the Infinity link. Close the ring **[N]**.

**15|** Repeat steps 11–14 on the opposite side of the chain mail segment, attaching it to a second Infinity link. Make sure this Infinity link is also positioned with the textured side up **[O]**.

**16|** Find the last set of rings on one side of the chain mail segment joining the Infinity links **[P]**.

**17|** Fold back this last set of rings **[Q]**. This will create V-shapes on either side of the chain mail segment, next to the Infinity links.

**18|** Pick up an open small ring and, as in steps 13 and 14, insert it behind the V-shape on one side and through the Infinity link on that side. Close the ring. Repeat for the V-shape on the opposite side. Repeat this process on the other end of the chain mail segment, folding back the last set of rings, and attaching the V-shapes to the Infinity links **[R]**.

**19|** Repeat steps 11–18 to join the nine Infinity links with the chain mail segments and then to attach the D-ring on each end of the bracelet. Make sure the Infinity links are all positioned with the textured side facing the same direction **[S]**.

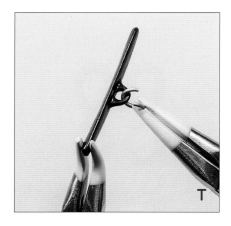

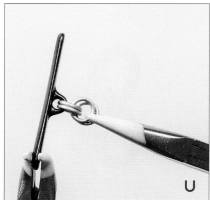

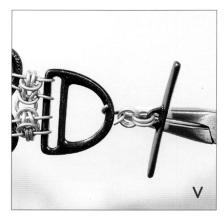

**20|** Pick up an open large ring and place it through the open loop of the toggle bar **[T]**. Close the ring. Add another open large ring beside it, following the same path, and close the ring. Pick up an open large ring and place it through the set of rings attached to the toggle bar. Close the ring. Add another open large ring beside it, following the same path, and close the ring **[U]**.

**21|** Pick up an open large ring, place it through the last set of rings attached to the toggle bar, and through the large opening in the D-ring on one side of your bracelet **[V]**. Close the ring.

**22|** Add another open large ring beside it, following the same path, and close the ring **[W]**. Depending on your preference, you can wear the finished bracelet with either the textured side or the smooth side of the Infinity links facing upward.

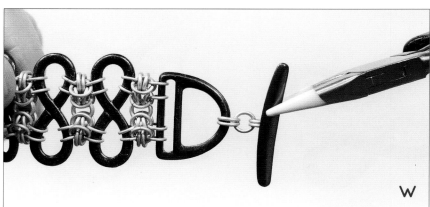

## Design Variations

- The black finish of the Infinity links looks amazing with nearly any ring color. Make all the chain mail segments in a single color (e.g. sky blue), you could alternate segment colors (e.g. sky blue between one set of links and lavender between the next), or make the segments in multiple colors to create a rainbow effect.

- Infinity links come in six different finishes, including antique silver, antique copper, and bright gold. D-rings are also available in several finishes. Make the bracelet with a single color of Infinity links or use several different finishes to create a mixed-metal bracelet.

- Try this design with other link components that can accommodate jump rings at multiple points along the sides.

# TRIPLE WRAP-SODY

This chain mail bracelet is based on the beaded leather triple-wrap bracelet, which is popular among celebrities and in beading and fashion magazines. These bracelets are usually made with 2mm leather cord and 4–6mm beads of various types. It occurred to me that these bracelets would also look great with chain mail in place of the beads. The helm chain worked nicely in providing a flat weave with the right balance of structure and flexibility for this design.

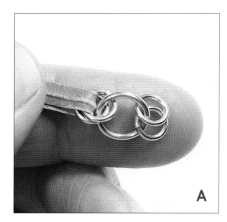

A

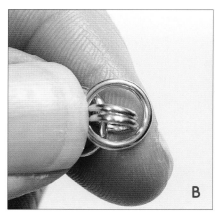

B

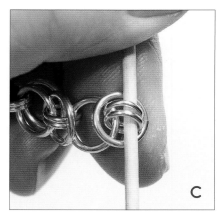

C

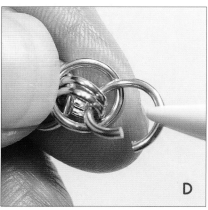

D

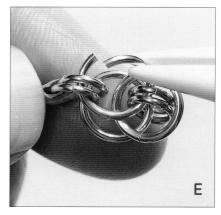

E

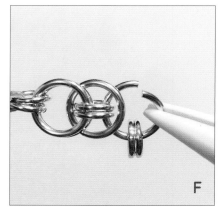

F

## MATERIALS »

*Bracelet size: 24" (61cm), which fits comfortably on a 7" (17.8cm) wrist.*

- Anodized aluminum jump rings
  - » **176** 16-gauge ¼" (6.7mm) ID, bright silver [AR 5.5]
  - » **121** 18-gauge ⁵⁄₃₂" (4.1mm) ID, bright silver [AR 4.1]
  - » **118** 20-gauge ⅛" (3.4mm) ID, bright silver [AR 4.2]
- 60" (152.4cm) of 2mm round leather cord, turquoise
- Flower of Life button, TierraCast, antique silver

## TOOLS »

- 2 pairs of pliers (chainnose, bent chainnose, and/or flatnose)
- Side cutters or sharp scissors
- Twist ties
- Toothpicks
- Ruler or tape measure

## MAKE THE CHAIN MAIL

**1|** To create the helm chain for the bracelet, you will use the 16-gauge ¼" rings (which we'll call the "large" rings) and the 18-gauge ⁵⁄₃₂" rings (which we'll call the "medium" rings). You will use the 20-gauge ⅛" rings (which we'll call the "small" rings) for attaching the leather cord.

Open 118 and close 58 large rings **(Chain Mail Techniques and Tips, p. 104)**. Open 1 and close 120 medium rings. Open all 118 small rings.

**2|** To start, pick up an open large ring with your pliers. Use that large ring to pick up four medium closed rings. Close the large ring. Arrange the medium rings so there are two rings on either side of the large ring. Place a twist tie through the two medium rings on one side. This will be your "handle" to help you hold and stabilize the weave **[A]**.

**3|** Place a closed large ring on top of the other two medium rings, so the large ring encircles the medium rings inside it **[B]**.

**TIP** If you're having difficulty holding the large ring in place encircling the medium rings, place a toothpick through the medium rings and over the top of the large ring **[C]**. This will help you hold everything in place until you attach the next ring, which will go through the medium rings and stabilize the large ring.

**4|** Pick up an open large ring and place it through the two medium rings encircled by the closed large ring. Make sure the open large ring doesn't go through the closed large ring, and that it sits above the closed large ring **[D]**.

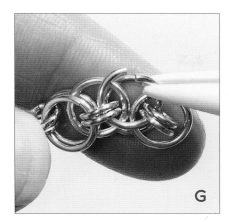

G

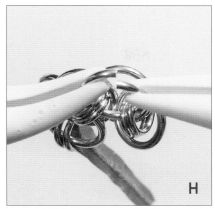

H

I

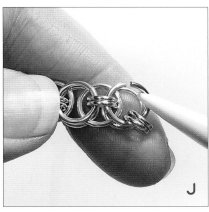

J

K

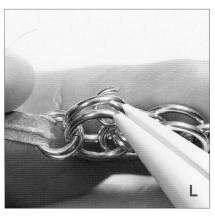

L

**5|** Still holding onto the open large ring, flip it to face the other direction and place it through the two medium rings on the other side. Make sure the open large ring doesn't pass through any other rings **[E]**. Close the ring.

**6|** Pick up an open large ring and use it to pick up two closed medium rings. Place the open large ring through the two medium rings at the end of your weave. Make sure the open large ring sits behind the closed large ring encircling the medium rings **[F]**. Close the ring.

**7|** Repeat steps 3–5. This time, when you place the open large ring through the two medium rings on the other side, be careful not to go through the encircling large ring on that side. Make sure the open large ring stays in front of this other encircling large ring **[G]**. Close the ring.

**TIP** It can be tricky to close the large ring after passing it through both sets of medium rings because the encircling rings on either side restrict some of the movement. In this case, start by closing the ring partially (enough to keep any rings from passing through the gap) **[H]**. Let go of the weave with one hand and let the rings re-settle into a new position. Then grasp the ring again with both sets of pliers and finish closing it **[I]**.

**8|** Repeat steps 3–7 until you have used all of the closed medium and large rings. You will not place an encircling large ring over the last set of medium rings. Pick up your last open large ring and pass it through the final set of medium rings and through the medium rings on the other side. Make sure not to pass through any other

rings and that the open large ring is in front of the last encircling large ring **[J]**. Close the ring.

**9|** Place a twist tie through the set of medium rings at the end of the weave **[K]**.

**10|** Go back to the beginning of the weave. Pick up an open small ring and pass it through the first set of two large rings **[L]**. Close the ring.

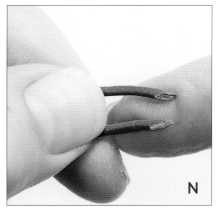

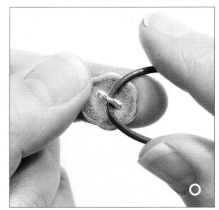

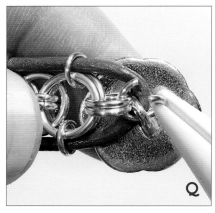

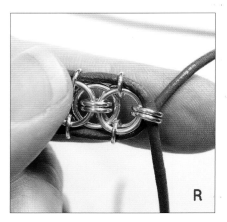

**11|** Repeat this step, placing small rings through each set of two large rings, on both sides of the bracelet for the full length of the weave **[M]**.

## ADD THE LEATHER CORD

**TIP** Use side cutters or sharp scissors to cut both ends of your leather cord at a sharp angle **[N]**. This will make it easier to pass the cord through the jump rings.

**1|** Insert the leather cord through the button shank. Center the button so it is at the midpoint of the leather cord **[O]**.

**2|** Starting at the beginning of the chain, insert one end of the leather cord through the small rings on one side of the bracelet. Insert the other end of the cord through the small rings on the other side of the bracelet **[P]**. Work the cord through the small

rings on both sides along the full length of the bracelet, until the button is positioned right in front of the first set of medium rings at the beginning of the bracelet.

**3|** Remove the twist tie from the beginning of the bracelet. Pick up the one remaining open medium ring, pass it through the button shank beside the leather cord, then through the two medium rings at the beginning of the bracelet **[Q]**. Close the ring.

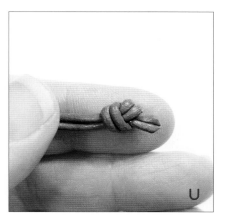

**4|** Remove the twist tie from the end of the bracelet. Pass the leather cord ends, in opposite directions, through the last set of medium rings on the bracelet **[R]**.

**5|** Bring both ends of the leather cord together and tie them into an overhand knot **(Basic Jewelry**

**Techniques, p. 110)** as close as possible to the last set of medium rings **[S]**.

**6|** Tie a second overhand knot further down the cords, leaving just enough room for the button to fit snugly between the two knots **[T]**.

**7|** Using your side cutters or sharp scissors, trim the excess from the leather cord ends. Depending on your preference, trim them close to the second knot or leave them longer. Or, cut them at an angle if you want a bit more of a decorative effect **[U]**.

## Design Variations
- Change the type of cord. For example, use 2mm satin cord or Chinese knotting cord.

- Change the length of the design to create a single- or double-wrap bracelet.

# NECKLACES

# FOREVER LAVENDER

This princess-length necklace drapes in a gentle curve just below the base of the neck. The beautiful Swarovski crystal pavé pendant is highlighted by the elegant simplicity of the chain mail and by the subtle pink arrows, pointing the way to infinity, amongst the lavender half-Byzantine weave.

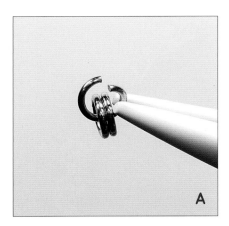

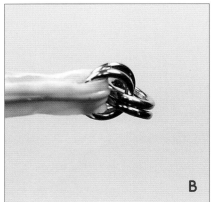

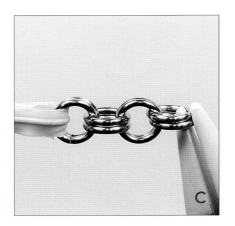

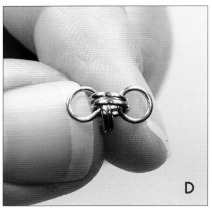

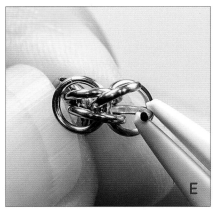

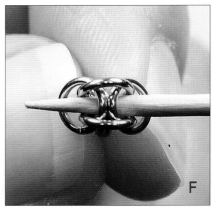

## MATERIALS >>

*Necklace size: 18¾" (47.6cm)*

- Anodized aluminum jump rings
  - » **250** 20-gauge ⅛" (3.4mm) ID, lavender [AR 4.2]
  - » **80** 20-gauge ⅛" (3.4mm) ID, pink [AR 4.2]
- 26mm crystal pavé Infinity pendant, Swarovski [67402], tanzanite and violet
- Melody toggle clasp, TierraCast, antique silver

## TOOLS >>

- **2** pairs of pliers (chainnose, bent chainnose, and/or flatnose)
- Twist ties
- Toothpicks

## MAKE THE NECKLACE

**1|** Close four of the lavender jump rings and open the remaining 246 lavender rings **(Chain Mail Techniques and Tips, p. 104)**. Open all 80 pink jump rings.

**2|** Pick up an open lavender ring and use it to pick up two closed lavender rings **[A]**. Close the ring.

**3|** Add another open lavender ring beside it, following the same path, and close the ring. Place a twist tie through one set of rings to use as a "handle" to hold and stabilize your weave **[B]**.

**4|** Pick up an open lavender ring and place it through the last set of two rings in the weave. Close the ring. Add another open lavender ring beside it, following the same path, and close the ring. Repeat to add a set of two pink rings to the last set of two lavender rings **[C]**.

**5|** Grasp the weave just below the set of pink rings. Fold back the pink rings, one to each side, so the previous set of lavender rings are sticking up in the middle **[D]**.

**6|** Pick up an open lavender ring, and insert it between the two lavender rings that are sticking up and through the pink rings you folded back **[E]**. Close the ring. Add another open lavender ring beside the first one, following the same path, and close the ring.

**TIP** If you're having difficulty getting the rings in position for this step, insert a toothpick between the two lavender rings that are sticking up in the middle and through the folded-back pink rings **[F]**. Use the toothpick to hold this pathway open while you insert the next ring. Once the ring is in place, remove the toothpick and close the ring.

G

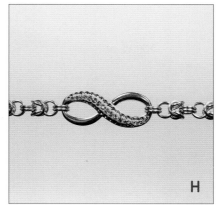

H

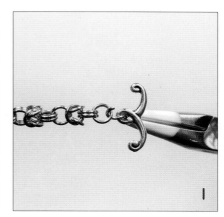

I

**7|** Continue the chain by adding two more sets of lavender rings (so you have three sets after the last pink rings). Then add a set of pink rings, fold back, and add a set of lavender rings as in steps 5 and 6. Repeat these steps until you have added a total of 20 sets of pink rings to your chain. Make sure to add three sets of lavender rings before each set of pink rings. Check your work: You should see the arrows formed by the pink rings are all pointing in the same direction and are equally spaced.

Fold back the last set of pink rings, and add a set of lavender rings through them. Next, pick up an open lavender ring, and place it through the last set of rings and through the loop on one side of the Infinity pendant. Close the ring. Add another open lavender ring beside it, following the same path, and close the ring **[G]**.

**8|** Repeat steps 2–7 to create a second chain and attach it to the other side of the pendant. On each side, the pink arrows should be pointing toward the pendant **[H]**.

**9|** Remove the twist tie from the last set of rings on one end of your necklace. Pick up an open lavender ring, and place it through the last set of rings and through the small loop on the toggle bar **[I]**. Close the ring. Repeat to attach the toggle ring to the other end of the necklace.

## Design Variations

- Make the necklace with 18-gauge ⁵/₃₂" (4.1mm) ID anodized aluminum jump rings. They are slightly larger rings with an AR of 4.1, so the weave will look nearly identical but will appear a bit heavier in relation to the pendant. It will also take fewer rings to create the same length.

- Change the colors of the rings. For example, use bright silver rings for most of the weave and lavender rings only for the "arrows." This will give the piece a much more subtle coloration.

- Change the focal pendant. This necklace can be made with numerous different types of oval or rectangular focal components, as long as you can attach a ring at each end. Swarovski crystal sew-on stones would be suitable for this design. TierraCast also makes many focal links and bezel links that would look great in this necklace. Gemstone beads and other types of beads could also be used: simply string a bead on a wire, make wrapped loops at both ends (Basic Jewelry Techniques, p. 110), and attach your jump rings to the wrapped loops.

# BLACK MAGIC

In this stylish black-and-silver necklace, a crystal pendant is framed by double-spiral chain mail attached to a quatrefoil link. Black satin ribbon woven through the necklace chain adds a touch of sophistication to the basic 1+2 weave.

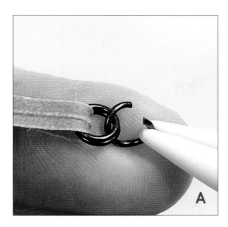

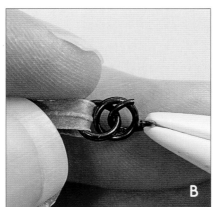

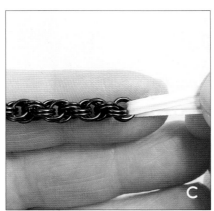

## MAKE THE PENDANT

**1|** To create the double-spiral chain for the pendant, you will use all 98 of the 4mm black-plated brass jump rings (which we'll call the "black rings"). Close two of these rings and open the other 96 rings **(Chain Mail Techniques and Tips, p. 104)**.

You will need two ³/₁₆" bright silver anodized aluminum jump rings (which we'll call the "large silver rings") and one ³/₃₂" bright silver anodized aluminum jump ring (which we'll call the "small silver ring"). Open both large silver rings and close the small silver ring.

**2|** To start your weave, place a twist tie through the two closed black rings. This will be a "handle" to help you hold and stabilize the weave. Pick up an open black ring and pass it through the two closed black rings **[A]**. Close the ring. Add another open black ring beside it, following the same path, and close the ring.

**3|** Position the last set of black rings so they overlap the previous set of rings to create an "eye." Make sure the second set of rings lies on top of the previous set of rings on the upper side of the eye (and they will also lie underneath the previous set of rings on the lower side of the eye).

Pick up an open black ring and pass it through the eye where the sets of

rings overlap **[B]**. Close the ring. Add another open black ring beside it, following the same path, and close the ring.

**TIP** For this weave, you may find it easier to insert the rings from the back side of the weave through to the front, rather than the usual method of inserting them from the front side of the weave through to the back. Try it both ways and see which method works best for you.

**4|** Repeat step 3 until you have used all but four of the black rings. Place a twist tie through the last set of rings **[C]**.

## MATERIALS >>

*Necklace size: 20" (51cm)*

- **98** 20-gauge 4mm (.149") ID jump rings, black-plated brass [AR 4.7]
- Anodized aluminum jump rings
  - » **68** 18-gauge ³/₁₆" (5mm) ID, bright silver [AR 5.0]
  - » **129** 20-gauge ³/₃₂" (2.4mm) ID, bright silver [AR 3.0]
- 32mm crystal Ellipse pendant, Swarovski [6470], jet
- Medium Quatrefoil link, TierraCast, bright rhodium
- Heirloom toggle clasp, TierraCast, black
- **24"** (61cm) of ¼" (6mm) wide satin ribbon, black
- **24"** (61cm) of polyester or nylon sewing thread, black

## TOOLS >>

- **2** pairs of pliers (chainnose, bent chainnose, and/or flatnose)
- Twist ties
- Scissors
- Hand-sewing needle
- Straight pin
- Ruler or tape measure

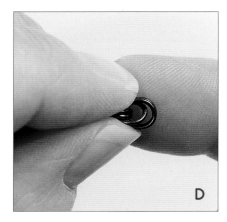

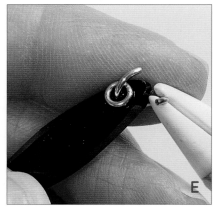

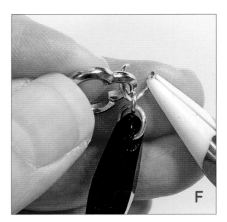

TIP If you're having difficulty keeping the "eye" open to insert the next set of rings, try pinching the rings between your thumb and forefinger after you have them in the correct postion [D].

5| Pick up an open large silver ring, and pass it through the hole of the Ellipse pendant and through the closed small silver ring [E]. Close the large ring.

6| Pick up the other open large silver ring, pass it through the small silver ring and the quatrefoil link [F], and then close the large ring.

7| Remove the twist tie from one end of the double-spiral chain. Insert an open black ring through the final set of rings at that end and also through the quatrefoil link immediately to the left of the large silver ring [G]. Close the ring. Add another open black ring

beside it, following the same path, and close the ring.

8| Remove the twist tie from the other end of your double-spiral chain. Insert an open black ring through the final set of rings at that end and, being careful not to twist the chain, bring it up the opposite side of the Ellipse pendant. Insert the ring through the quatrefoil link immediately to the right of the large silver ring [H]. Close the ring.

Add another open black ring beside it, following the same path, and close the ring. You have now finished the pendant for your necklace [I].

## COMPLETE THE NECKLACE

1| To create the necklace, you will need 66 large silver rings: 64 for the necklace chain and two to attach the pendant. Open all of the large silver rings.

You will also need 128 of the small silver rings. Close 126 of these for the necklace chain and open two of them for attaching the toggle clasp.

2| Pick up an open large silver ring, pass it through two closed small silver rings, and close the large ring. Place a twist tie through the large silver ring [J].

3| Pick up another open large silver ring, use it to pick up two closed small silver rings, and pass it through the two small rings attached to the previous ring [K]. Close the large ring.

4| Repeat step 3 until you have used all but two of the large silver rings and all but two of the small silver rings. Your chain should end with a large silver ring. Place a twist tie through the last ring [L].

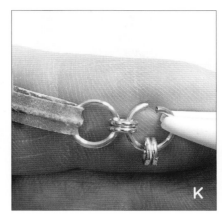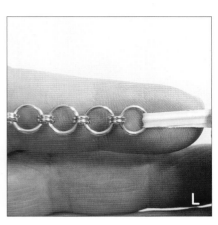

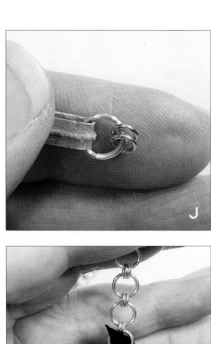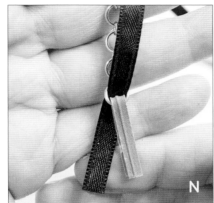

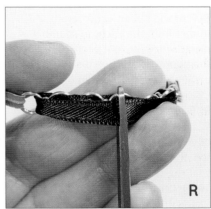

**5|** Use scissors to cut one end of your satin ribbon at a slant, as this will make it easier to weave it through your chain. Insert the beveled end of the ribbon through the first large ring at one end of your chain, from the back side of the chain through to the front **[M]**. Pull the ribbon through the ring until there is only about 1" (2.5cm) remaining **[N]**.

**6|** Weave the satin ribbon through the chain by inserting it through each large ring, weaving from the front side to the back in one ring **[O]**, then from the back side to the front in the next ring **[P]**. Make sure the 1" of ribbon remains at the end and doesn't get pulled through the chain. Pull the ribbon snug at each weave, but not so tight the chain starts to buckle, before moving on to the next ring. Check that your ribbon is remaining straight, and not twisting, at each weave **[Q]**.

**7|** At one end of your necklace, fold the remaining ribbon to the back side of the necklace. Cut the remaining ribbon length to ¾" (19mm) **[R]**.

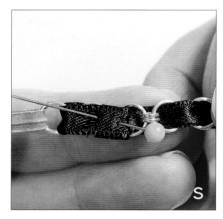

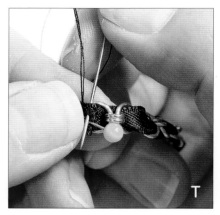

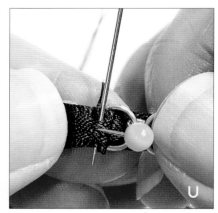

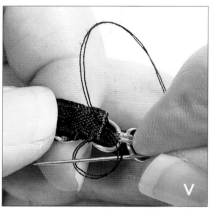

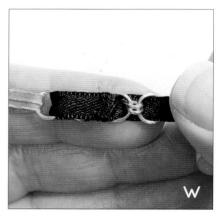

8| Fold the ribbon under itself ¼" (6mm) from the end and secure it in place with a straight pin [S]. Folding the ribbon under before sewing will prevent fraying of the cut end.

9| Thread your sewing needle with 12" (30cm) of thread. Align the ends of your thread evenly and knot them together.

10| On the upper ribbon edge near the folded end, push your needle through the two layers of the folded ribbon, starting from behind the ribbon and pushing the needle towards you [T]. Pull the needle and thread through the ribbon (this will secure your knot between the layers of ribbon so it won't show on the front of your necklace).

Make three or four more stitches on the upper ribbon edge, close to the first stitch, going through all three layers of the ribbon for these stitches. For each stitch, push the needle through from behind the ribbon and toward you. Make sure

the needle and thread don't pass through any of the jump rings of your chain.

11| Make a stitch across the ribbon to bring your needle out near the lower edge of the ribbon [U]. Make three or four stitches on the lower ribbon edge, going through all three layers of the ribbon. For each stitch, push the needle through from behind the ribbon and towards you. Again, make sure not to catch any of the jump rings in your stitches.

12| Remove the straight pin. Push the needle through the folded edge of the ribbon, and pull the thread through until there is a small loop remaining. Pass your needle through this loop [V], and pull the thread tight. This is a half-hitch knot. Tie two more half-hitch knots through the folded end of the ribbon, then cut the thread close to the last knot.

13| Repeat steps 7–12 to sew and secure your ribbon at the other end of your necklace [W].

14| Pick up an open small silver ring, insert it through the loop of one piece of your toggle clasp and through the last ring on one end of your necklace [X]. Close the ring. Repeat at the other end of the necklace to attach the other half of the toggle clasp.

15| Position your necklace so the front side is facing you (i.e. the sewn ribbon ends are on the underside). Locate the middle set of two small rings that show on the front of the necklace (there should be 15 sets on either side of it). Pick up one of the two remaining open large silver rings, and insert it below the two small rings, following the same path as the small rings [Y]. Close the ring.

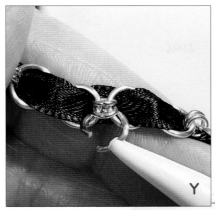

**16|** Position the ring you just attached to the necklace so the upper side of the ring lies on top of the rings on either side. Pick up the last open large silver ring, pass it through the quatrefoil link and through the lower side of the ring you attached to the necklace **[Z]**. Close the ring.

## Design Variations

- Change the length of the necklace. If making the necklace chain longer, make sure you still end up having both ends of the ribbon folding back to the same side, and you still have a center point to attach the pendant.

- Try using other long and narrow pendants, and adjust the length of your double-spiral chain to provide the right fit. Keep in mind the Ellipse pendant is 5/16" (8mm) wide. If you choose a pendant that is wider, the double spiral chain might not hang properly at the sides of the pendant.

- Change the type of ribbon or cord to weave through the necklace. Try other 3/16–1/4" (5–6mm)-wide ribbons or cords, as long as they are thin, flexible, and can be sewn at the ends. It would be interesting to see if flat leather or suede cord would work for this necklace.

# JUST BEACHIN'

This necklace celebrates summer at the beach and the beautiful color palette inspired by sand, sea, and sky. The European 4-in-1 chain mail weave creates a lovely drape around the neck in shades of blue, green, gold, and bronze. The clasp and the beach-themed charm, crystal, and pearl embellishments take center stage as the frontal piece of this necklace.

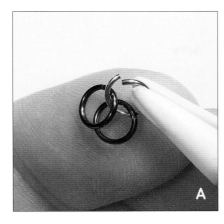

A

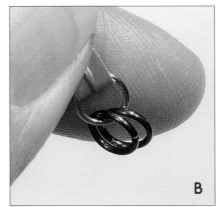

B

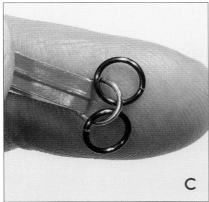

C

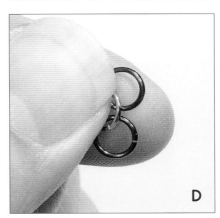

D

## MATERIALS >>

*Necklace size: 21½" (54.6cm)*

- Anodized aluminum jump rings
    - » **98** 20-gauge ⁵/₃₂" (4.3mm) ID, gold [AR 5.3]
    - » **190** 20-gauge ⁵/₃₂" (4.3mm) ID, bronze [AR 5.3]
    - » **81** 20-gauge ⁵/₃₂" (4.3mm) ID, seafoam [AR 5.3]
    - » **81** 20-gauge ⁵/₃₂" (4.3mm) ID, sky blue [AR 5.3]
    - » **44** 20-gauge ⁵/₃₂" (4.3mm) ID, royal blue [AR 5.3]
- 20mm crystal Starfish pendant, Swarovski [6721], aquamarine
- Xilion bicone crystal beads, Swarovski [5328]
    - » **2** 6mm, smoked topaz
    - » 6mm, Pacific opal
    - » 4mm, smoked topaz
    - » **2** 4mm, Pacific opal
    - » **2** 4mm, aquamarine
- **2** 4–5mm freshwater potato pearls, light blue
- **12** 21-gauge 2" (5.1cm) headpins, brass
- **3** charms, 1 each of Seahorse, Seastar, and Spindle Shell, TierraCast, antique gold
- **2** Shell beads, TierraCast, antique gold
- Toggle clasp, Heirloom, TierraCast, antique gold

## MAKE THE NECKLACE

**1|** You will use all of the bronze and gold jump rings to create the core row of the necklace base. Close all 190 of the bronze rings and open all 98 of the gold rings (you will use 96 of these rings for the necklace base and two to attach the toggle clasp) **(Chain Mail Techniques and Tips, p. 104)**.

**2|** Pick up an open gold ring and use it to pick up two closed bronze rings **[A]**.

**3|** Close the gold ring and place a twist tie through it. This will be your "handle" to help you hold and stabilize the weave **[B]**.

**4|** Position the bronze rings so the side of the bronze rings closest to the twist tie lies on top of the gold ring and the side of the gold ring farthest away from the twist tie lies on top of the bronze rings **[C]**.

E

**5|** Once you have these rings in position, pinch them slightly between your thumb and forefinger to hold them in place **[D]**.

**6|** With your other hand, pick up an open gold ring and use it to pick up two closed bronze rings **[E]**.

## TOOLS >>

- **2** pairs of pliers (chainnose, bent chainnose, and/or flatnose)
- Twist ties
- Roundnose pliers
- Side cutters

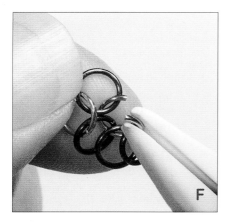

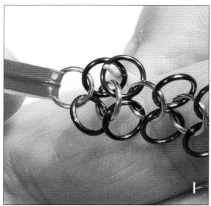

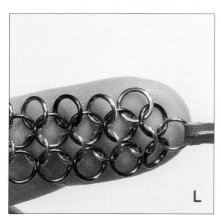

**7|** Pass the open gold ring through the bronze rings you are pinching in position: through the front side of the bottom ring and up through the back side of the top ring. Make sure you don't go through the previous gold ring **[F]**. Close the ring.

**8|** Positioning the newly added rings as you did in step 4, you can see the weave configuration starting to take shape **[G]**.

**9|** Repeat steps 5–8 until you have a total of 96 gold rings on your chain. When adding the last gold ring (the 96th), do not pick up and add two bronze rings with it—add the gold ring only. Close the last gold ring, and place a twist tie through it **[H]**. You have now completed the core of the necklace weave.

**10|** You are now going to widen the chain mail weave by adding a row of rings to each side. To start, place 75 sky blue rings, 75 seafoam rings, and 38 royal blue rings into a single pile and "stir them" a bit to blend them together. (We'll call these the "mix" rings.) Open all of these rings.

**11|** Return to the starting point of your necklace. Make sure the gold rings are angled down on the left side and angled up on the right side. If they are angled the other way, flip the weave over. On the upper row of bronze rings, note how the second ring overlaps the first, creating an "eye"

(where the toothpick is inserted) **[I]**. This eye occurs all along this row, for each pair of adjacent rings. You will be inserting the new row of rings through these eyes.

**12|** Pick up an open mix ring. Pass it from front to back through the second ring in the upper row and then from front to back through the first ring in the upper row. This places the ring through the eye where the first two rings in the upper row overlap **[J]**. Close the ring.

**13|** Pick up an open mix ring and pass it from front to back through the next (the third) ring in the upper row and then from front to back through the previous (the second) ring in the upper row. This places the ring through the next eye in the upper row **[K]**. Close the ring.

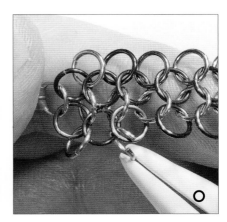

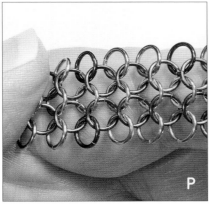

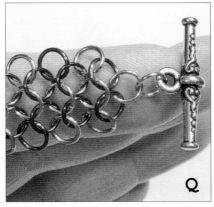

**14|** Repeat step 13 until you reach the end of the upper row of bronze rings **[L]**.

**15|** Return to the starting point of your necklace. On the lower row of bronze rings, an eye occurs for each pair of adjacent rings (where the toothpick is inserted), just as in the upper row of rings **[M]**. You will be inserting another new row of rings through these eyes.

**16|** Pick up an open mix ring. Pass it from back to front through the first ring in the lower row and then from back to front through the second ring in the lower row. This places the ring through the eye where the first two rings in the lower row overlap **[N]**. Close the ring.

**17|** Pick up an open mix ring and pass it from back to front through the last ring (the second) you passed through in the lower row and then from back to front through the next (the third) ring in the lower row. This places the ring through the next eye in the lower row **[O]**. Close the ring.

**18|** Repeat step 17 until you reach the end of the lower row of bronze rings **[P]**.

**19|** At this point, you should have two open gold rings left from the original batch of 98. At one end of the necklace, remove the twist tie. Pick up an open gold ring and place it through the gold ring at the end of the necklace and through the small loop of one piece of your toggle clasp. Close the ring **[Q]**. Repeat at the other end of your necklace to attach the other half of your toggle clasp. You have now completed the necklace base.

## ADD THE EMBELLISHMENTS

**1|** For each of the Swarovski crystals, pearls, and Shell beads, insert a headpin through the bead, and make a wrapped loop at the other end **(Basic Jewelry Techniques, p. 110) [R]**.

**2|** You should have six sky blue rings, six seafoam rings, and six royal blue rings remaining. Open all of these rings.

Pick up an open royal blue ring, place it through the hole in the Starfish pendant, and close the ring. Pick up an open sky blue ring, attach the royal blue ring, and close it.

Position your necklace so the toggle ring is to the left side. Pick up an open seafoam ring, place it through the sky blue ring at the end of the Starfish dangle, and then through the toggle ring. Close the seafoam ring [S].

3| Pick up an open sky blue ring, place it through the wrapped loop on one of the Shell beads, and close the ring. Pick up an open seafoam ring, place it through the wrapped loop of the 6mm pacific opal crystal, and then through the sky blue ring. Close the seafoam ring. Pick up an open royal blue ring, put it through the wrapped loop of the 4mm smoked topaz crystal, and then through the seafoam ring [T].

4| Holding your toggle ring and necklace in the same position as in step 2, place the royal blue ring through the toggle ring to the left of the Starfish pendant. Make sure to position the smoked topaz crystal to the front side of the dangle. Close the royal blue ring [U].

5| Pick up an open royal blue ring, place it through the Seastar charm, and close the ring. The Seastar charm has a distinctive front and back, just like a real seastar. You can choose which side you want to display on

your necklace [V, W]. I think the back side (photo W) is more detailed and interesting, so I will keep it facing to the front as I build and attach this dangle.

6| Pick up an open seafoam ring, place it through the wrapped loop of one of the pearls, and then through the royal blue ring attached to the Seastar charm. Close the seafoam ring. Pick up an open sky blue ring, place it through the wrapped loop of one of the 4mm aquamarine crystals, and then through the seafoam ring that has the pearl attached to it [X].

7| Position your toggle ring and necklace as in step 2. Place the sky blue ring of your Seastar dangle through the first mix ring closest to the toggle in the bottom row of the necklace. Make sure your Seastar charm is facing the way you want it to display. Also make sure the aquamarine crystal is sitting on the front side of the dangle (not the back). When

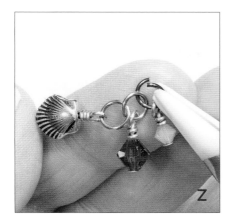

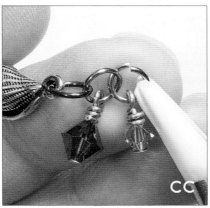

this is all placed correctly, close the sky blue ring **[Y]**.

**8|** Pick up an open sky blue ring, place it through the wrapped loop of the remaining shell bead, and close the ring. Pick up an open seafoam ring, place it through the wrapped loop of one of the 6mm smoked topaz crystals, and then through the sky blue ring. Close the seafoam ring. Pick up an open royal blue ring, place it through the wrapped loop of one of the 4mm Pacific opal crystals, and then through the seafoam ring **[Z]**.

**9|** Place the royal blue ring of your Shell bead dangle through the mix ring that is five rings to the right of the ring where you attached the Seastar dangle in the bottom row of the necklace. In other words, there should be four "empty" rings between the rings where the dangles are attached.

Make sure the Pacific opal crystal is sitting on the front side of the dangle (not the back). Close the royal blue ring **[AA]**.

**10|** You have now attached all the dangles to the toggle ring side of your necklace **[BB]**. Next, you will attach the dangles to the toggle bar side.

**11|** Pick up an open royal blue ring, place it through the Spindle Shell charm, and close the ring. Pick up an open sky blue ring, place it through the wrapped loop of the remaining 6mm smoked topaz crystal, and then through the royal blue ring. Close the sky blue ring. Pick up an open seafoam ring, place it through the wrapped loop of the remaining 4mm aquamarine crystal, and then through the sky blue ring **[CC]**.

**12|** Position your necklace so the toggle bar is to the right side. Make

sure the bottom side, where you will be attaching the dangles, is the same side of the necklace as where you attached the dangles on the toggle ring side. Place the seafoam ring of your Spindle Shell dangle through the second mix ring to the left of the toggle bar in the bottom row of the necklace. Make sure the aquamarine crystal is sitting on the front side of the dangle (not the back). Close the seafoam ring **[DD]**.

**13|** Pick up an open seafoam ring, place it through the Seahorse charm, and close the ring. Pick up an open royal blue ring, place it through the wrapped loop of the remaining pearl, and then through the seafoam ring. Close the royal blue ring. Pick up an open sky blue ring, place it through the wrapped loop of the remaining 4mm Pacific opal crystal, and then through the royal blue ring **[EE]**.

**14|** Place the sky blue ring of your Seahorse dangle through the mix ring that is five rings to the left of the ring where you attached the Spindle Shell dangle in the bottom row of the necklace. In other words, there should be four "empty" rings between the rings where the dangles are attached.

Turn the dangle so the Seahorse is facing toward the toggle bar. Make sure the Pacific opal crystal is sitting on the front side of the dangle (not the back). Close the sky blue ring **[FF, GG]**.

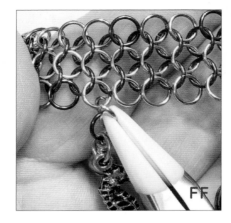

## Design Variations

- Change the theme of the necklace. For example, create a Christmas theme, a Halloween theme, or a Valentine's Day theme (as pictured below). Change the charms and embellishments of your dangles and the colors of your rings to match your theme.

- Change the width of the necklace. For example, make the necklace narrower (as in the Valentine's Day necklace pictured below) by completing the core row of the necklace base and omitting the additional rows of rings you added to the top and bottom of the weave in the main project.

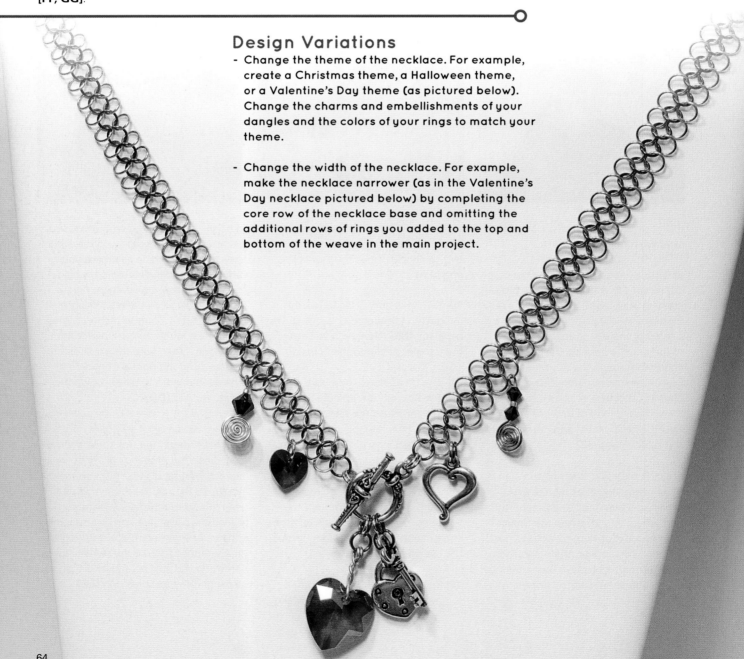

# ELVEN PRINCESS

Warm earthtones of browns and greens unite in this lush celebration of woodland spring, featuring vines of queen's braid chain mail joining antique copper components and crystals. Perhaps in another time and place, this design would grace the neck of an elven princess as she danced at the festival of the vernal equinox.

*Necklace size: 21½" (54.6cm)*

- **691** 20-gauge ⁵⁄₃₂" (4.3mm) ID anodized aluminum jump rings, seafoam [AR 5.3]
- **20** 20-gauge small oval .083x.125" (2.11x3.18mm) ID jump rings, copper
- **2** 8mm crystal clover beads, Swarovski [5752], emerald
- Xilion bicone crystal beads, Swarovski [5328]
  - » **2** 6mm, emerald
  - » **2** 4mm, emerald
  - » **2** 6mm, Pacific opal
  - » **2** 4mm, Pacific opal
  - » 6mm, smoked topaz
  - » **2** 4mm, smoked topaz
- **13** 21-gauge 2" (5.1cm) headpins, copper
- Leaf focal link, TierraCast, antique copper
- **3** Oak Leaf charms, TierraCast, antique copper
- **2** Braided 3-1 links, TierraCast, antique copper
- Toggle clasp, 3 Leaf, TierraCast, antique copper
- 4" (10.2cm) of 3x2mm curb chain, antique copper

## TOOLS >>

- **2** pairs of pliers (chainnose, bent chainnose and/or flatnose)
- Toothpicks
- Roundnose pliers
- Side cutters

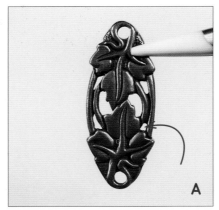

A

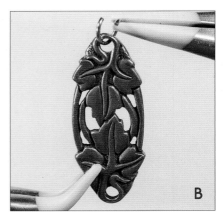

B

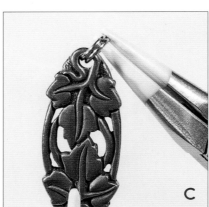

C

D

## MAKE THE NECKLACE

**1|** For the chain mail sections attaching the leaf focal link to the 3-1 links, you will need 54 of the seafoam jump rings for each of the two shorter chains and 82 rings for each of the two longer chains. For the chain mail sections attaching the 3-1 links to the toggle clasp, you will need 209 rings for the chain to the toggle ring and 210 rings for the chain to the toggle bar. Open all 691 seafoam rings. Open all 20 small oval copper jump rings **(Chain Mail Techniques and Tips, p. 104)**. You will use seafoam rings until step 21.

**2|** Position the leaf focal link with the front side facing toward you so the smallest of the inner holes is situated on the bottom right-hand side **[A]**. This is important, as it will ensure your chain mail sections sit evenly on each side of the focal link.

**3|** Keeping your focal link in position, pick up an open ring and place it through the round hole at the top of the focal link **[B]**. Close the ring.

**4|** Add another open ring beside it, following the same path, and close the ring **[C]**.

**5|** Pick up an open ring and place it through the set of rings attached to the focal link. Close the ring. Add another open ring beside it, following the same path, and close the ring **[D]**.

E

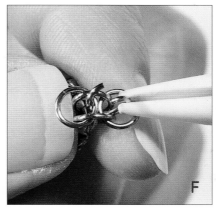

F

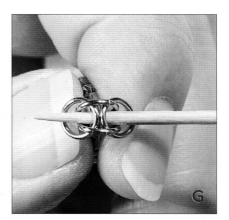

G

H

I

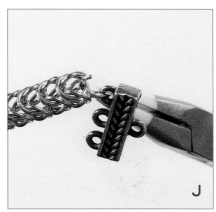

J

K

**6|** Grasp your weave just below the set of rings you just added. Fold back the last set of rings, one to each side, so the previous set of rings are sticking up in the middle **[E]**.

**7|** Pick up an open ring, and insert it between the two rings that are sticking up in the middle, and through the rings that you folded back **[F]**. Close the ring.

TIP If you're having difficulty getting the rings in position for this step, insert a toothpick between the two rings that are sticking up in the middle and through the folded-back rings **[G]**. Use the toothpick to hold this pathway open while you insert the next ring. Once the ring is in place, remove the toothpick and close the ring.

**8|** Add another open ring beside it, following the same path, and close the ring **[H]**.

**9|** Pick up an open ring and place it through the set of rings you just added. Close the ring. Add another open ring beside it, following the same path, and close the ring **[I]**.

**10|** Repeat steps 6–9 until you have used 52 rings. Fold back your last set of rings, place an open ring through them (as in step 7), and then through the leftmost loop of one of the 3-1 links **[J]**. Close the ring.

**11|** Add another open ring beside it, following the same path, and close the ring. Position your piece as pictured, with the chain mail angling upward and to the right of the focal link **[K]**.

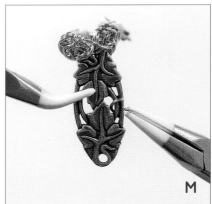

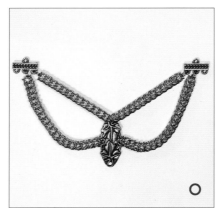

**12|** Go back to the focal link and repeat steps 3–10 to create another chain. This time, after you have used 52 jump rings, fold back your last set of rings, place an open ring through them (as in step 7), and then through the rightmost loop of the other 3-1 link. Close the ring. Add another open ring beside it, following the same path, and close the ring. Position your piece as pictured, with the new chain angling upward and to the left of the focal link **[L]**.

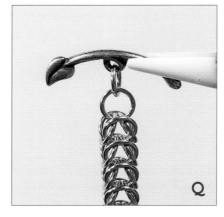

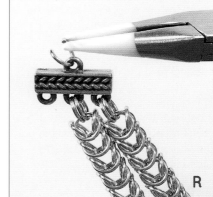

**13|** Go back to the focal link. Pick up an open ring and place it through the largest of the three holes in the middle right side of the link **[M]**. Close the ring. Add another open ring beside it, following the same path, and close the ring.

Repeat steps 5–9 until you have used 80 jump rings. Fold back your last set of rings, place an open ring through them (as in step 7), and then through the middle loop of the 3-1 link on the right side. Before attaching to

the 3-1 link, make sure your weave isn't twisted and both chains on the right side are in the same alignment. Close the ring. Add another open ring beside it, following the same path, and close the ring.

**14|** Go back to the focal link. Repeat step 13 on the left side of the link, creating a chain from the largest of the three holes in the middle left side of the link **[N]** to the middle loop of the 3-1 link on the left side. Again, before

attaching to the 3-1 link, make sure your weave isn't twisted and both chains on the left side are in the same alignment.

**15|** You've attached the focal link to the 3-1 links. When you lay your weave out, you should see a nice draping of the lower chains **[O]**.

**16|** Pick up an open ring and place it through the single loop on the 3-1 link on the right side **[P]**. Close the

ring. Add another open ring beside it, following the same path, and close the ring.

**17|** Repeat steps 5–9 until you have used 208 jump rings. Fold back your last set of rings, place an open ring through them (as in step 7), and close the ring. Pick up an open ring, and place it through the ring you just added and through the open loop of the toggle bar. Close the ring **[Q]**.

**18|** Pick up an open ring and place it through the single loop on the 3-1 link on the left side **[R]**. Close the ring. Add another open ring beside it, following the same path, and close the ring.

**19|** Repeat steps 5–9 until you have used 208 jump rings. Fold back your last set of rings, place an open ring through them (as in step 7) and through the small loop of the toggle ring. Close the ring **[S]**.

**20|** String each Swarovski crystal bead on a headpin, and make a wrapped loop at the other end (**Basic Jewelry Techniques, p. 110**) **[T]**.

**21|** Cut four pieces of chain with your side cutters: one piece that is nine links in length and three pieces that are each six links in length.

Pick up an open oval copper ring, place it through the last link at one end of the nine-link piece of chain, then through the round hole at the bottom of the focal link. Close the ring. Pick

up an open oval ring, place it through the last link at the other end of the nine-link piece of chain, then through the wrapped loop of an emerald clover bead. Close the ring. Lay the piece flat and straighten the chain, so you can tell which is the left and which is the right side of the chain links. Using open oval rings, attach the wrapped loops of the following beads to the left side of this chain: a 4mm Pacific opal crystal to the third link from the top, a 6mm emerald crystal to the fifth link from the top, and the 6mm smoked topaz crystal to the seventh link from the top. Close each ring after attaching the crystal to the chain, before moving on to the next one.

Pick up an open oval copper ring, place it through the last link at one end of a six-link piece of chain, then through the round hole at the bottom of the focal link, making sure it sits to the right of the nine-link chain. Close the ring. Pick up an open oval ring, place it through the last link at the other end of the six-link piece of chain, then through the wrapped loop of an emerald clover bead. Close the ring. Lay the piece flat and straighten the chain, so you can tell which is the left and which is the right side of the chain links. Using open oval rings, attach the wrapped loops of the following beads to the right side of this chain: an Oak Leaf charm to the first link at the top, a 4mm emerald crystal to the third link from the top, and a 6mm Pacific opal crystal to the fifth link from the top. Close each ring after attaching

the component to the chain before moving on to the next one **[U]**.

**22|** Pick up an open oval copper ring, place it through the last link at one end of a six-link piece of chain, then through the rightmost loop of the 3-1 link on the right side of the necklace. Close the ring. Pick up an open oval ring, place it through the last link at the other end of the six-link piece of chain, then through an Oak Leaf charm. Close the ring. Lay the piece flat and straighten the chain so you can see which is the left and right side of the chain links.

Using open oval rings, attach the wrapped loops of the following beads to this chain: a 4mm smoked topaz crystal to the left side of the first link at the top, a 6mm emerald crystal to the right side of the third link from the top, and a 4mm Pacific opal crystal to the left side of the fifth link from the top. Close each ring after attaching the crystal to the chain, before moving on to the next one **[V]**.

W

**23|** Pick up an open oval copper ring and place it through the last link at one end of a six-link piece of chain, then through the leftmost loop of the 3-1 link on the left side of the necklace. Close the ring. Pick up an open oval ring and place it through the last link at the other end of the six-link piece of chain, then through an Oak Leaf charm. Close the ring. Lay the piece flat and straighten the chain, so you can tell which is the left and which is the right side of the chain links.

Using open oval rings, attach the wrapped loops of the following beads to this chain: a 4mm emerald crystal to the right side of the first link at the top, a 6mm Pacific opal crystal to the left side of the third link from the top, and a 4mm smoked topaz crystal to the right side of the fifth link from the top. Close each ring after attaching the crystal to the chain before moving on to the next one **[W]**.

## Design Variations

- **Add more or fewer chains and beads**

- **Add longer dangles for a dramatic effect.**

- **Try gemstone beads, Czech fire-polished beads, or pearls either in place of, or in addition to, the Swarovski crystals.**

# JEWELRY SETS

# QUEEN OF THE NILE

Swarovski crystal scarab beads and golden double-spiral chain mail take center stage in this Egyptian-themed bracelet and earrings set, with a 4-in-2 weave forming the bracelet end pieces. In ancient Egypt, scarab beetles were associated with the Egyptian god, Khepri, who pushed the sun across the sky. Scarabs made from carved stone (such as jasper, amethyst, or carnelian) or molded from ceramic were often used as amulets or incorporated into jewelry. I can picture an ancient Egyptian queen wearing this jewelry as she floats on her royal barge down the Nile.

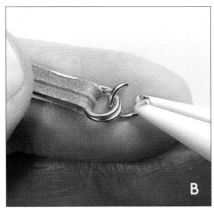

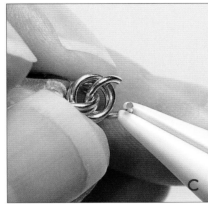

## MAKE THE BRACELET

**1|** String a scarab bead on an eyepin and make a plain loop at the other end **(Basic Jewelry Techniques, p. 110) [A]**; make the plain loop as close to the same size as the eyepin loop as you can. You have now made a scarab bead link. Repeat with three more scarab beads for a total of four scarab links. Set these links aside for now.

**2|** You will use 96 4mm gold-plated brass jump rings (which we'll call the "small gold rings") to create the double-spiral chains for the central section of the bracelet. Close two of these rings and open the other 94 rings **(Chain Mail Techniques and Tips, p. 104)**.

For the end sections of the bracelet, you will use 12 ³⁄₁₆" gold anodized aluminum jump rings (which we'll call the "large gold rings") and 72 ³⁄₁₆" royal blue anodized aluminum jump rings (which we'll call the "large blue rings"). Open all of the large gold and large blue rings. You will use 70 ³⁄₃₂" royal blue anodized aluminum jump rings (which we'll call the "small blue rings"). Open six of the small blue rings and close the other 64 rings.

You will need an additional four small gold rings (one closed and three open) to attach the toggle clasp.

**3|** You will create three pieces of double-spiral chain mail for the central section of the bracelet. To start the first piece, insert a twist tie through two closed small gold rings. This will form a "handle" that will help you hold and stabilize the weave. Pick up an open small gold ring and place it through the two closed rings **[B]**. Close the ring. Add another open small gold ring beside it, following the same path, and close the ring.

**4|** Position the two sets of small gold rings so that they overlap to create an "eye." Make sure the second set of rings lies on top of the previous set of rings on the upper side of the eye (they will also lie underneath the previous set of rings on the lower side of the eye). Pick up an open small gold ring and pass it through the eye where the sets of rings overlap **[C]**. Close the ring. Add another open small gold ring beside it, following the same path, and close the ring.

## MATERIALS >>

*Bracelet size: 7⅞" (20cm), which fits snugly on a 7" (17.8cm) wrist (a snug fit helps keep the scarab beads from flipping over)*

- **100** 20-gauge 4mm (.149") ID jump rings, gold-plated brass [AR 4.7]
- Anodized aluminum jump rings
  - » **72** 18-gauge ³⁄₁₆" (5.0mm) ID, royal blue [AR 5.0]
  - » **12** 18-gauge ³⁄₁₆" (5.0mm) ID, gold [AR 5.0]
  - » **70** 20-gauge ³⁄₃₂" (2.4mm) ID, royal blue [AR 3.0]
- **4** 12mm crystal scarab beads, Swarovski [5728], scarabaeus green
- **4** 21-gauge 2" (5cm) eyepins, brass
- Sunburst toggle clasp, TierraCast, antique gold

*Earring size: 2⅝" (6.7cm)*

- **192** 20-gauge 4mm (.149") ID jump rings, gold-plated brass [AR 4.7]
- **4** 18-gauge ³⁄₁₆" (5.0mm) ID anodized aluminum jump rings, royal blue [AR 5.0]
- **2** 12mm crystal scarab beads, Swarovski [5728], scarabaeus green
- **2** 21-gauge 2" (5cm) headpins, brass
- Pair of gold-filled regular loop earring wires

## TOOLS >>

- **2** pairs of pliers (chainnose, bent chainnose, and/or flatnose)
- Twist ties
- Roundnose pliers
- Side cutters

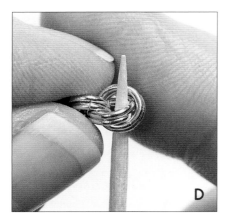

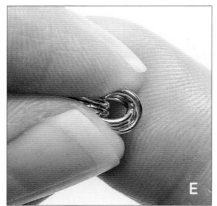

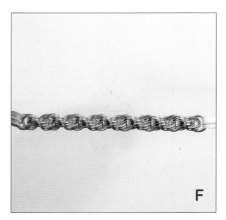

**TIP** This is a fairly tight weave, so if you are having difficulty getting the eye open, try inserting a tooth-pick through it **[D]**. Once you have the eye open, remove the toothpick, and pinch the rings slightly be-tween your thumb and first finger to keep them in the correct position while you insert the next ring **[E]**.

**TIP** For double-spiral weave, you may find it easier to insert the rings from the back side of the weave through to the front, rather than the usual method of inserting them from the front side of the weave through to the back. I suggest that you try it both ways and see which method works best for you.

**5|** Repeat step 4 until you have used 60 of the small gold rings. Place a twist tie through the last set of rings in the chain **[F]**.

**6|** Pick up one of your scarab bead links. Pick up an open small gold ring and place it through the open loop at the head end of the scarab bead **[G]**. Close the ring.

**7|** Add another open small gold ring beside it, following the same path, and close the ring **[H]**. This set of two closed small gold rings will be the start of the second piece of double-spiral chain mail for the central section of the bracelet.

**8|** Repeat steps 3 and 4 to create double-spiral chain mail, starting at the two closed rings attached to the scar-ab bead link. Continue until you have used a total of 16 open small gold rings. Pick up an open small gold ring, pass it through the eye of the previous two sets of rings and then through the open loop at the head end of another one of your scarab bead links **[I]**. Close the ring. Add another

open small gold ring beside it, following the same path, and close the ring.

**9|** Repeat steps 6–8 to create another piece of double-spiral chain mail with a scarab bead link at each end. This is the third, and final, piece for the central section of your bracelet **[J]**.

**10|** Next, create the two end sections of your bracelet. Start by picking up an open large blue ring and use it to pick up two closed small blue rings **[K]**. Close the ring. Add another open large blue ring beside it, following the same path, and close the ring.

**11|** Pick up an open large blue ring and use it to pick up two closed small blue rings. Place the open large blue ring through the rightmost small blue ring on the previous set of large blue rings. Make sure that the open large blue ring doesn't pass through the closed large blue rings **[L]**. Close the ring.

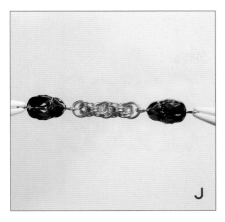

J

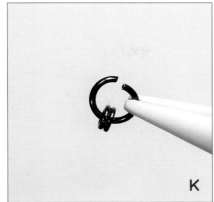

K

L

M

N

O

**12|** Add another open large blue ring beside it, following the same path through the three small blue rings, but not through any other large blue ring. Close the ring **[M]**.

**13|** Pick up an open large blue ring and use it to pick up a closed small blue ring. Place the open large blue ring through the rightmost of the two loose small blue rings on the previous set of large blue rings. Make sure that the open large blue ring doesn't pass through the closed large blue rings **[N]**. Close the ring.

**14|** Add another open large blue ring beside it, following the same path through the two small blue rings, but not through any other large blue ring. Close the ring **[O]**. You have completed the first row of the end section. You should have three sets of two large blue rings joined together by a small blue ring between each set.

Each of the sets of large blue rings should also have a loose small blue ring attached.

**15|** Turn the weave so that the first row sits vertically, with the loose small blue rings on the right. Pick up an open large blue ring and use it to pick up two closed small blue rings. Place the open large blue ring through the loose small blue ring on the bottom set of large blue rings of the previous row **[P]**. Close the ring. Add another open large blue ring beside it, following the same path through the three small blue rings, but not through any other large blue ring. Close the ring.

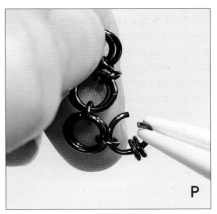

P

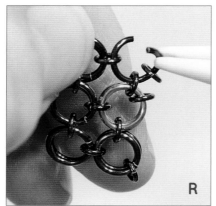

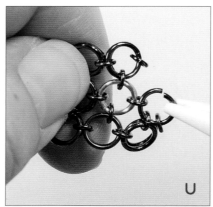

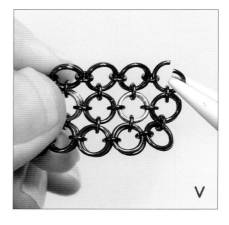

**16|** Pick up an open large gold ring and use it to pick up two closed small blue rings. Place the open large gold ring through the uppermost of the two loose small blue rings on the just-added set of large blue rings and through the loose small blue ring on the middle set of large blue rings in the previous row **[Q]**. Close the ring.

Add another open large gold ring beside it, following the same path through the four small blue rings, but not through any other large ring. Close the ring.

**17|** Pick up an open large blue ring and use it to pick up a closed small blue ring. Place the open large blue ring through the uppermost of the two loose small blue rings on the set of large gold rings and through the loose small blue ring on the last set of large blue rings in the previous row **[R]**. Close the ring. Add another open large blue ring beside it, following the same path through the three small blue

rings, but not through any other large ring. Close the ring.

**18|** Repeat steps 15–17 until you have completed six rows. For the middle set of rings in each row, alternate between using large blue rings in one row and large gold rings in the next row. Your last row should have large gold rings as the middle set **[S]**.

**19|** For the final row, pick up an open large blue ring and use it to pick up a closed small blue ring. Place the open large blue ring through the loose small blue ring on the bottom set of large blue rings of the previous row **[T]**. Close the ring. Add another open large blue ring beside it, following the same path through the two small blue rings, but not through any other large blue ring. Close the ring.

**20|** Pick up an open large blue ring and use it to pick up a closed small blue ring. Place the open large blue ring through the loose small blue ring on

the just-added set of large blue rings and through the loose small blue ring on the middle set of large gold rings in the previous row **[U]**. Close the ring.

Add another open large blue ring beside it, following the same path through the three small blue rings, but not through any other large ring. Close the ring.

**21|** Pick up an open large blue ring and, without picking up any closed small blue rings, place it through the loose small blue ring on the just-added set of large blue rings and through the loose small blue ring on the upper-most set of large blue rings in the previous row **[V]**. Close the ring.

Add another open large blue ring beside it, following the same path through the two small blue rings, but not through any other large ring. Close the ring.

**22|** This completes one end section of your bracelet. Repeat steps 10–21 to create a second end section.

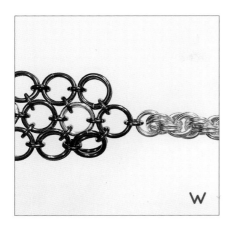

W

X

Y

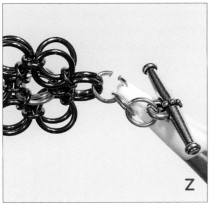

Z

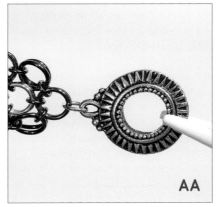

AA

BB

**23|** Now you will attach the central and end sections together. Remove the twist ties from the ends of your first piece of double-spiral chain mail (this will be the longest section, with no scarab bead links). Pick up one of the six open small blue rings, and place it through the set of rings at one end of the double-spiral weave and through the middle set of large blue rings in the final row of one of your end sections. Close the ring **[W]**.

**24|** Pick up another open small blue ring. Place it through the open loop at the back end of one of your scarab bead link sections and through the bottom set of large blue rings in the final row of the end section. Close the ring. Repeat to attach the other scarab bead link section to the uppermost set of large blue rings in the final row of the end section **[X]**.

**25|** Repeat steps 23 and 24 to attach the other end of the central section to the other end section.

**TIP** You may find it difficult to close the small blue rings when using them to connect the central and end sections of your bracelet. If you wish, use small gold rings in place of the small blue rings for joining the sections. In this case, you need to make this switch for all six of the connecting rings. Remember also that you will need six more small gold rings and six fewer small blue rings than what is listed in the materials section.

**26|** Pick up an open small gold ring. Place it through a closed small gold ring and through the loop on the toggle bar of the clasp **[Y]**. Close the ring.

**27|** Pick up an open small gold ring. Place it through the closed small gold ring farthest from the toggle bar and through the middle set of large blue rings in the final row at one end of your bracelet **[Z]**. Close the ring.

**28|** Pick up the last open small gold ring. Place it through the loop on the toggle ring of your clasp and through the middle set of large blue rings in the final row of the other end of your bracelet. Close the ring **[AA]**.

## MAKE THE EARRINGS

**1|** Insert a headpin through one of the scarab beads, so that the head of the pin is at the back end of the bead. Make a wrapped loop at the head end of the scarab bead, positioning the loop so that the circle of the loop is facing the side of the bead **[BB]**.

**2|** For each earring, you will use 96 of the small gold rings to create the double-spiral chains. Close six of these rings and open the other 90 rings. Open two large blue rings as well.

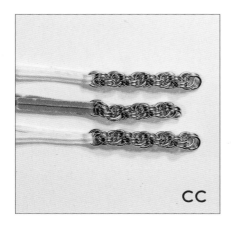

**3|** Follow steps 3 and 4 of the bracelet instructions to create three double-spiral chains: one chain with 28 small gold rings, and two chains with 34 small gold rings each **[CC]**.

**4|** Position the double-spiral chains so that the short chain is in the middle and the longer chains are on either side of it. Pick up an open large blue ring. Place it through the last set of rings in each of the double-spiral chains, in the order that you have

positioned them, and then through the wrapped loop on the scarab bead **[DD]**. Close the ring.

**5|** Remove the twist ties from the starting ends of the double-spiral chains. Pick up an open large blue ring. Place it through the starting set of rings in each of the double-spiral chains, in the order that you have positioned them, and through the loop of an earring wire **[EE]**. Close the ring.

Make sure the chains aren't twisted and the earring wire is positioned so the scarab bead faces toward the front of the earring.

**6|** Repeat to make a second earring.

## Design Variations

- Replace the Swarovski crystal scarab beads with other beads that are 12mm long and no more than 8mm wide, such as Swarovski crystal mini drop beads [5056].

- Eliminate the beads and make the three double-spiral chains the same length (60 rings). Or, alternate the ring colors for these chains. For example, make the middle chain with 4mm gold-plated brass jump rings, and make the two outside chains with 4mm black-plated brass jump rings.

- Make the earrings with only the center piece of double-spiral chain (rather than three pieces). In this case, use small blue rings as the connectors, rather than the large blue rings.

# MADE WITH LOVE

Sky-blue European 4-in-1 weave, edged with soft pink, forms the foundation of this bracelet and earring set. Embellished with links and charms that express adoration and devotion, this jewelry is indeed made with love.

## MATERIALS >>

*Bracelet size: 7¾" (19.7cm), which fits comfortably on a 7" (17.8cm) wrist*

- Anodized aluminum jump rings
    - » **237** 18-gauge ⁵/₃₂" (4.1mm) ID, sky blue [AR 4.1]
    - » **82** 18-gauge ⁵/₃₂" (4.1mm) ID, pink [AR 4.1]
- Love focal link, TierraCast, antique silver
- **2** charms, Heart Lock and Key, TierraCast, antique silver
- Jubilee toggle clasp, TierraCast, antique silver

*Earring size: 2³/₈" (6cm)*

- Anodized aluminum jump rings
    - » **22** 18-gauge ⁵/₃₂" (4.1mm) ID, sky blue [AR 4.1]
    - » **18** 18-gauge ⁵/₃₂" (4.1mm) ID, pink [AR 4.1]
- **2** Jubilee Heart charms, TierraCast, antique silver
- Pair of sterling silver earring wires

## TOOLS >>

- **2** pairs of pliers (chainnose, bent chainnose and/or flatnose)
- Twist ties
- Toothpicks

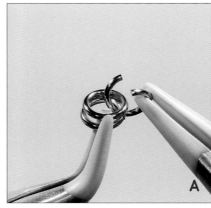
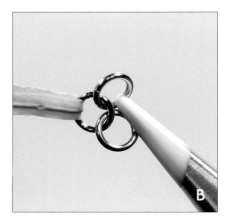
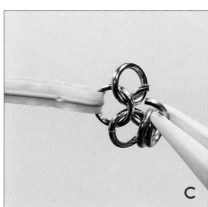
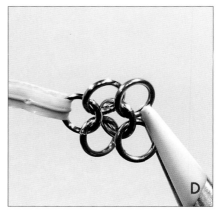

## MAKE THE BRACELET

**1|** For the bracelet, close 132 of the blue rings and open the remaining 105 blue rings **(Chain Mail Techniques and Tips, p. 104)**. Close eight of the pink rings and open the remaining 74 pink rings.

**2|** Pick up an open pink ring and use it to pick up two closed pink rings **[A]**.

**3|** Close the ring and place a twist tie through it, to use as a "handle" to hold and stabilize your weave. Position your triplet of rings so the left side of the first pair of rings lies on top of the single ring, and the right side of the single ring lies on top of the pair of rings **[B]**.

**4|** Pick up an open blue ring and use it to pick up two closed blue rings. Pass the open blue ring through the previous pair of rings: through the front side of the bottom ring and up through the back side of the top ring. Make sure you don't go through the single ring from the previous step **[C]**. Close the blue ring.

**5|** Positioning the newly added rings as you did in step 3, you can see the weave configuration starting to take shape **[D]**.

**6|** Repeat steps 4 and 5 until you have a total of 35 "triplets" (a single ring plus a pair of rings) on your chain: one pink triplet plus 34 blue triplets.

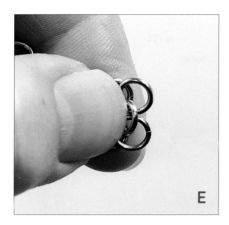

E

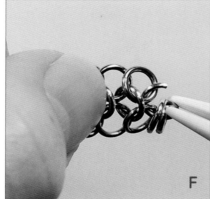

F

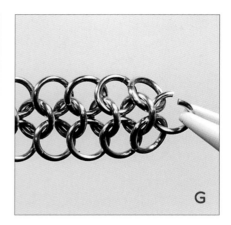

G

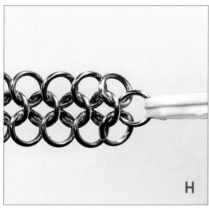

H

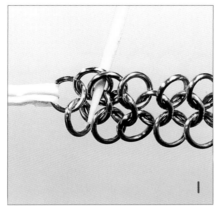

I

J

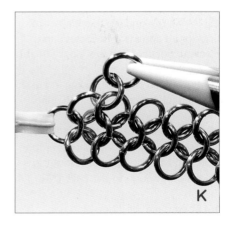

K

TIP To keep the rings in the proper position as you're adding a new triplet of rings, first flip the rings in the last triplet in your chain into the correct position. Then, pinch the triplet slightly between your thumb and forefinger, just behind the right edge of the single ring. Hold them in this position until you have added your next triplet **[E]**.

**7|** For the final triplet, pick up an open blue ring and use it to pick up two closed pink rings. Follow steps 4 and 5 to add the last triplet to the chain **[F]**.

**8|** Pick up an open pink ring, but this time, do not pick up any other rings with it. Pass the open pink ring through the previous pair of rings: through the front side of the bottom ring and up through the back side of the top ring **[G]**.

**9|** Close the pink ring and attach a twist tie to it **[H]**. You have finished

the base row of your bracelet. The next step is to add rows on the sides.

**10|** Return to the starting point of your base row. Make sure that the single rings of your triplets are angled down on the left side and angled up on the right side. This is the front side of the bracelet. If they are angled the other way, flip the weave over. On the top row of rings, note how the second ring overlaps the first, creating an "eye" (where the toothpick is inserted) **[I]**. This eye occurs all along this row, for each pair of adjacent rings.

**11|** Pick up an open pink ring and use it to pick up a closed pink ring. Pass the open pink ring through the eye where the first two rings in the top row overlap **[J]**. Close the ring.

**12|** Notice how the two rings you just added form a triplet with the first blue ring in the top row. Position the rings in this triplet as in step 3 **[K]**.

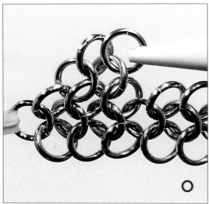

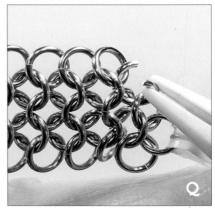

**13|** When the rings in this triplet are positioned correctly, hold them in place as described in the Tip, p. 81 **[L]**.

**14|** Pick up an open blue ring and use it to pick up a closed blue ring. Find the blue ring in the top row that is to the immediate right of the triplet you are holding in position. Place the open blue ring through this ring, from the front side through to the back **[M]**.

**15|** Then pass the open blue ring through the pair of rings in the triplet you are holding in position: through the front side of the bottom ring and up through the back side of the top ring **[N]**. Close the ring.

**16|** You have created a new triplet, which consists of the two rings you added plus the blue ring on the right that they passed through. Position your new triplet as in step 3 **[O]**.

**17|** Repeat steps 13–16 until you reach the last blue ring in the top

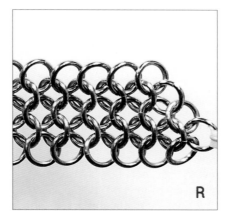

row. When adding rings to create a triplet with this last blue ring, pick up a closed pink ring (rather than a closed blue ring) for step 14, then continue through as usual to step 16 **[P]**.

**18|** Pick up an open pink ring, but this time, do not pick up any other rings with it. Pass through the last pink ring in the top row, as in step 14. Then, pass through the last triplet as in step 15 **[Q]**.

**19|** Close the ring **[R]**.

**20|** Return to the starting point of your weave. Make sure the weave is positioned with the front side of the bracelet facing you (see step 10).

As in the top row of rings, the bottom row also has "eyes" (where the toothpick is inserted) where each pair of adjacent rings overlap **[S]**.

**21|** Pick up an open pink ring and use it to pick up a closed pink ring. Pass

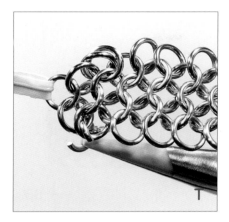

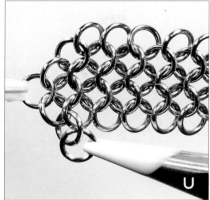

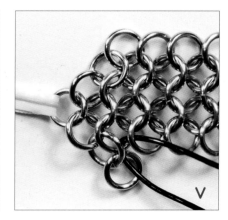

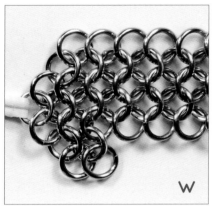

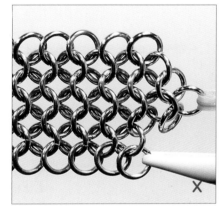

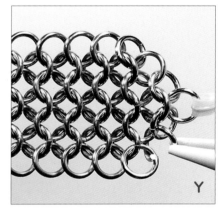

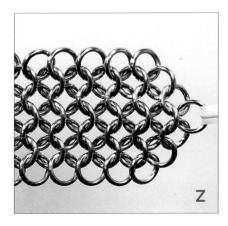

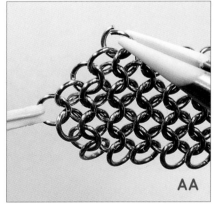

the open pink ring through the eye where the first two rings in the bottom row overlap. (The closed ring is sitting behind the weave right now, so it is difficult to see in this picture **[T]**.) Close the open pink ring.

**22]** The two rings you just added form a triplet with the first blue ring in the bottom row. Position the rings in this triplet as in step 3 **[U]**.

**23]** Hold the triplet in position as described in the Tip, p. 81. Pick up an open blue ring and use it to pick up a closed blue ring. Pass the open blue ring through the pathway shown by the black wire **[V]**. First, pass the open blue ring through the pair of rings in the triplet (through the front side of the bottom ring and up through the back side of the top ring). Then, pass the open blue ring through the blue ring in the bottom row to the immediate right of the triplet, from the back side of this ring to the front.

**24]** You have created a new triplet, which consists of the two rings you added plus the blue ring on the right that they passed through. Position your new triplet as in step 3 **[W]**.

**25]** Repeat steps 23 and 24 until you reach the last blue ring on the bottom row. To create a triplet with the last blue ring, pick up a closed pink ring (rather than a closed blue ring) in step 23, then continue to step 24 **[X]**.

**26]** Pick up an open pink ring, but this time, do not pick up any other rings with it. Pass it through the last triplet, then through the last pink ring in the bottom row, as in step 23 **[Y]**.

**27]** Close the ring **[Z]**.

**28]** Return to the starting point of your weave. Make sure the front side of the bracelet is facing you (see step 10).

Pick up an open pink ring and pass it through the eye where the first two rings in the top row overlap **[AA]**. Close the ring.

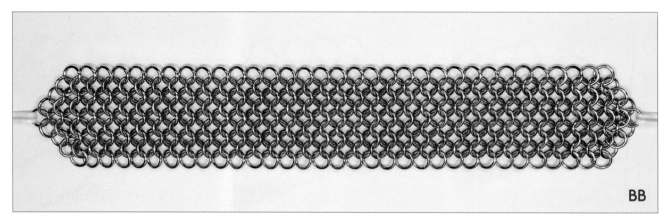
BB

CC

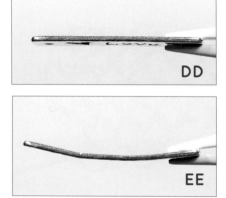
DD

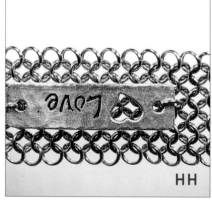
EE

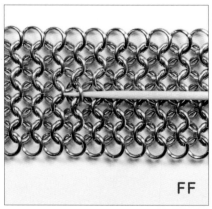
FF

GG

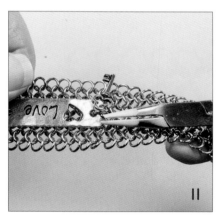
HH

II

**29|** Continue along the top row, placing open pink rings though the eye of each pair of adjacent rings, then closing the rings. Repeat this process along the bottom row. You have now completed the foundation for your bracelet **[BB]**.

**30|** Pick up the love focal link **[CC]**.

**31|** Turn it sideways, and you will see that it is flat **[DD]**. Work the focal link

with your fingers to bend it into a slight curve **[EE]**. This will make it conform better to the shape of your wrist.

**32|** Lay the bracelet flat, with the front side up. In the middle row of rings, find the fourteenth ring from the left (this will be the thirteenth blue ring from the left). Place a toothpick through the right side of this ring **[FF]**.

**33|** Pick up an open blue ring and place it through the hole that is closest to the letter "e" in the focal link. Remove the toothpick and place the open blue ring through the right side of the fourteenth ring **[GG]**. Close the ring.

**34|** Moving to the right from the fourteenth ring in the center row, count over nine more rings, to the twenty-third ring from the left. Pick up an open blue ring, put it through the

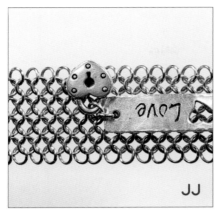

JJ

KK

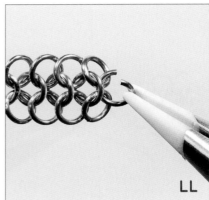

LL

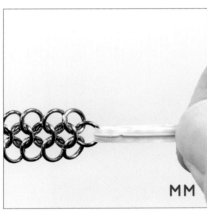

MM

NN

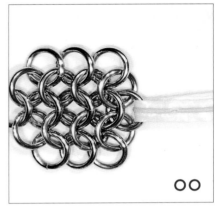

OO

right side of the twenty-third ring, and then through the hole in the other side of the focal link. Close the ring **[HH]**.

TIP The focal link is attached upside-down, so that it will appear right-side up when worn on the right wrist with the arm facing downward and with the toggle bar on the left side (which I find is easier to fasten with one hand). You can certainly change this.

**35|** Pick up an open blue ring and pass it through the Heart Key charm and then through the ring that goes through the right side of the focal link **[II]**. Close the ring.

**36|** Repeat to attach the Heart Lock charm to the other side of the focal link **[JJ]**.

**37|** Pick up an open pink ring and place it through the loop on the toggle bar. On the left side of your bracelet (the starting end), remove the twist tie and put the open pink ring through the ring that had the twist tie **[KK]**. Close the ring. Repeat to attach the toggle ring to the other side of the bracelet.

## MAKE THE EARRINGS

**1|** For each earring, you will use 11 blue rings (six closed and five open) and nine pink rings (two closed and seven open).

**2|** Repeat steps 2–5 of the bracelet instructions. Then repeat steps 4 and 5 until you have a total of four triplets: one pink triplet and three blue triplets. Pick up an open blue ring, but this time, do not pick up any other rings with it. Pass the open blue ring through the previous pair of rings: through the front side of the bottom ring and up through the back side of the top ring **[LL]**.

**3|** Close the ring and attach a twist tie to it **[MM]**.

**4|** Return to the starting point of the weave. Pick up an open pink ring and place it through the eye where the first two rings in the top row overlap **[NN]**. Close the ring.

**5|** Continue along the top row, putting open pink rings though the eye of each pair of adjacent rings, then closing the rings. Then repeat this process along the bottom row. You should have three pink rings along the edges of both the top and bottom rows **[OO]**.

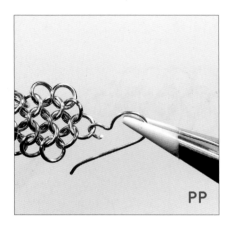

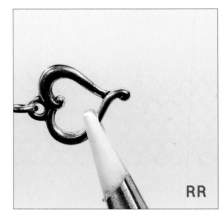

**6|** Open the bottom loop of an earring wire as you would a jump ring. Return to the starting point of the weave, remove the twist tie from the top pink ring, and place this ring inside the open earring wire loop **[PP]**. Close the loop.

**7|** Remove the twist tie from the bottom blue ring of the earring. Pick up an open blue ring, and connect the

small loop of the Jubilee Heart charm and the bottom blue ring. Make sure the small swirl at the bottom of the charm is pointing to the right **[QQ]**. Close the ring.

**8|** Repeat to make a second earring. When attaching the Jubilee Heart charm to this earring, turn the charm so the bottom swirl is pointing to the left **[RR]**.

## Design Variations

- If you don't want an "edging" effect, make the entire bracelet in a single color. If you want more color variation, alternate colors for each row, make each row a different color, or try other color combinations.

- There are many other links and charms that are suitable to attach to this bracelet base. If you want more than a single focal link, space out 3–5 smaller connector links on the front of the bracelet, either with or without attaching additional charms.

- Add more embellishments to the bracelet. For example, attach small Swarovski crystals (4–6mm bicones, rondelles, etc.) at several points on the front of the bracelet. To do this, string a crystal on a headpin and make a wrapped loop at the other end (Basic Jewelry Techniques, p. 110). Then, attach it to one of the rings in the bracelet base with a jump ring.

- Make the bracelet without any charms or other embellishments and let your chain mail weave take center stage.

# PINK CHAMPAGNE

This multi-drop necklace and earring set combines queen's braid and flower weaves. The color mix of champagne and dark rose in the chain mail complements the queen baguette crystals. When I close my eyes, I can imagine wearing this jewelry while sitting on a deck overlooking the ocean, watching an amazing sunset, and, of course, sipping pink champagne.

*Necklace size: 20" (50.8cm)*

- Anodized aluminum jump rings
  - » **15** 16-gauge ¼" (6.7mm) ID, champagne [AR 5.5]
  - » **270** 20-gauge ⁵⁄₃₂" (4.3mm) ID, champagne [AR 5.3]
  - » **287** 20-gauge ⁵⁄₃₂" (4.3mm) ID, dark rose [AR 5.3]
- **5** 25x7mm crystal Queen Baguette pendants, Swarovski 6465, crystal paradise shine
- Hammertone Ellipse toggle clasp, TierraCast, oxidized brass

*Earring size: 2½" (6.4cm)*

- Anodized aluminum jump rings
  - » **6** 16-gauge ¼" (6.7mm) ID, champagne [AR 5.5]
  - » **20** 20-gauge ⁵⁄₃₂" (4.3mm) ID, champagne [AR 5.3]
  - » **22** 20-gauge ⁵⁄₃₂" (4.3mm) ID, dark rose [AR 5.3]
- **2** 25x7mm crystal Queen Baguette pendants, Swarovski 6465, crystal paradise shine
- Pair of regular loop gold-filled earring wires, TierraCast

- **2** pairs of pliers (chainnose, bent chainnose, and/or flatnose)
- Twist ties
- Toothpicks

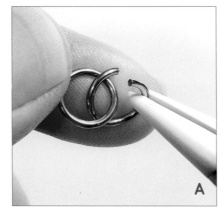

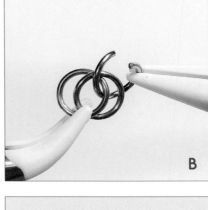

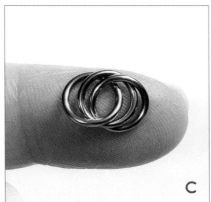

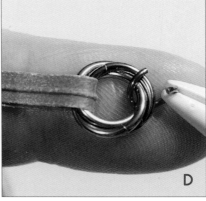

## MAKE THE NECKLACE

**1|** You will be making flower links with the ¼" champagne jump rings (which we'll call the "large rings"). You will be making queen's braid chain with the ⁵⁄₃₂" champagne and dark rose rings (which we'll call the "champagne rings" and the "pink rings").

Open 10 large rings and close five large rings **(Chain Mail Techniques and Tips, p. 104)**. Open all of the 270 champagne rings and all of the 287 pink rings.

**2|** Pick up an open large ring and use it to pick up a closed large ring. Position the rings so that they overlap to create an "eye." Make sure that the ring on the right lies on top of the left ring on the upper side of the eye (it will also lie underneath the left ring on the lower side of the eye) **[A]**. Close the ring.

**3|** Pick up an open large ring and place it through the eye you created with the previous two rings. Make sure this new ring lies on top of the previous rings on the upper side of the eye **[B]**. Close the ring.

**4|** You have now created a flower link. Each ring in the link should lie on top of the ring to its left on the upper side of the eye **[C]**. Move or flip the rings if necessary to get them into this position.

**5|** Once the rings are in the correct position, place a twist tie through the eye of the rings to hold them in place.

Pick up an open pink ring and place it through the flower link. Close the ring. Add another open pink ring beside it, following the same path **[D]**, and close the ring.

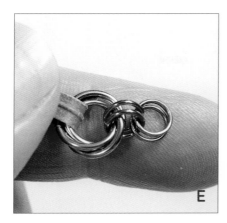

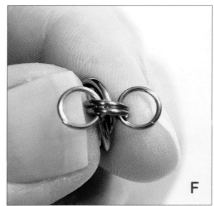

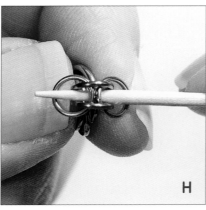

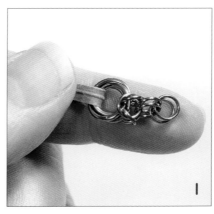

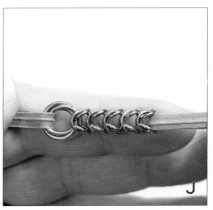

**6|** Pick up an open champagne ring and place it through the two pink rings. Close the ring. Add another open champagne ring beside it, following the same path, and close the ring **[E]**.

**7|** Grasp the weave just below the champagne rings you just added. Fold the champagne rings back, one to each side, so that the pink rings are sticking up in the middle **[F]**.

**8|** Pick up an open pink ring, insert it between the two pink rings, and through the champagne rings that you folded back **[G]**. Close the ring. Add another open pink ring beside it, following the same path, and close the ring.

TIP If you're having difficulty getting the rings in place for this step, insert a toothpick between the two pink rings and through the folded-back champagne rings **[H]**. Use the toothpick to hold this

pathway open while you insert the next ring. Once the ring is in place, remove the toothpick and close the ring.

**9|** Pick up an open champagne ring and place it through the two pink rings you just added. Close the ring. Add another open champagne ring beside it, following the same path, and close the ring **[I]**.

**10|** Repeat steps 7–9 until you have added a total of five sets of pink rings and five sets of champagne rings to the weave. After adding the last set of champagne rings, fold them back and insert a twist tie (rather than two pink rings), **[J]** as in step 8.

**11|** Repeat steps 2–10 until you have a total of five segments. These will be the drops for the front of the necklace. The next step is to join these segments together.

**12|** Pick one of these segments to be the center point of your necklace. Hold it upright, with the flower link at the top. Pick up an open pink ring and place it through the link on the right side, between the twist tie at the top and the chain mail weave at the bottom. Close the ring. Add another open pink ring beside it, following the same path, and close the ring **[K]**.

89

L

M

N

**13|** Repeat steps 6–9 until you have added a total of five sets of pink rings and five sets of champagne rings. Fold back the last set of champagne rings. Insert an open pink ring as in step 8 and pass this open ring through the left side of the flower link of another completed segment. Close the ring. Add another open pink ring beside it, following the same path, and close the ring **[L]**.

**14|** As in step 12, add a set of pink rings to the right side of the flower link in the segment you just added **[M]**. Follow step 13 to continue the weave and attach it to another completed segment. You now have three completed segments linked together: the center segment and the two right-hand segments.

**15|** Go back to your center segment. As in step 12, add a set of pink rings to the flower link in the center segment, but this time, add them to the left side of the center segment **[N]**. Flip your weave around so the center link is on the right and the two added segments are on the left. Repeat steps 13 and 14 to add the remaining two completed segments to your weave. You now have all five completed segments linked together.

**16|** Go to the last segment on the right of the weave. Add a set of pink rings on the right side of the flower link of this segment. Repeat steps 6–9 until you have added a total of 45 sets of pink rings and 45 sets of

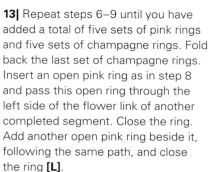

O

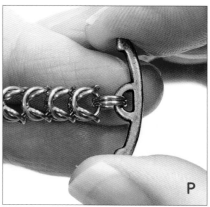

P

champagne rings. Fold back the last set of champagne rings. Insert an open pink ring as in step 8 and also pass this open ring through the small hole in the toggle ring of the clasp. Close the ring. Add another open pink ring beside it, following the same path, and close the ring **[O]**.

**17|** Go to the last segment on the left of the weave. Add a set of pink rings on the left side of the flower link of this segment. Repeat steps 6–9 until you have added a total of 45 sets of pink rings and 45 sets of champagne rings. Fold back the last set of champagne rings. Insert an open pink ring as in step 8 and also pass this open ring through the hole in the toggle bar of the clasp. Close the ring. Add another open pink ring beside it, following the same path, and close the ring **[P]**.

Q

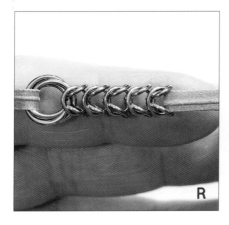

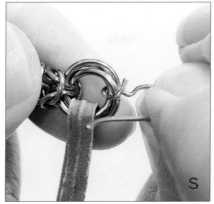

**18|** At the bottom of each of the five segments on the front of your necklace, remove the twist tie and insert an open pink ring in its place. Connect one of the pendants, and then close the ring **[Q]**. Remove any additional twist ties remaining on your necklace.

## MAKE THE EARRINGS

**1|** For each earring, you will need three large rings (one closed and two open), 10 champagne rings (all open), and 11 pink rings (all open).

**2|** Follow steps 2–10 from the necklace instructions to complete a segment with a flower link and queen's braid chain mail **[R]**.

**3|** Open the bottom loop of an earring wire as you would a jump ring. Place the flower link inside the open loop, making sure you have all three rings of the flower link fully inside the loop **[S]**. Close the loop. Remove the twist tie from the flower link.

**4|** At the bottom of the earring, remove the twist tie and insert an open pink ring. String a pendant on the pink ring, and then close it **[T]**.

**5|** Repeat to make a second earring.

## Design Variations

- Change the length of the drop segments, either shorter or longer, depending on your preference.

- Change the type of pendant. For example, Swarovski crystal spike pendants will give this necklace an edgier look, while pear or teardrop pendants will create a softer look.

# RED CARPET

Golden double-spiral chain mail is fashioned into a teardrop shape that frames a ruby crystal, forming the pendant and drops for this necklace and earrings set. The simple European 4-in-1 weave of the necklace chain is embellished with red satin ribbon, creating the appearance of lace edging. These elements come together in a luxurious design befitting a red carpet premiere.

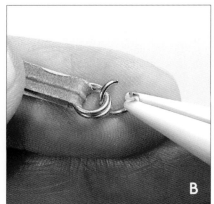

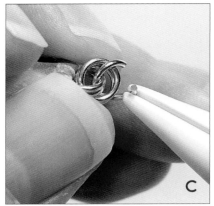

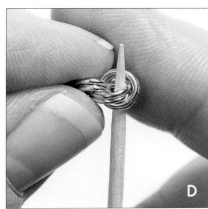

## MAKE THE PENDANT

**1|** You will use 78 of the 4mm gold-plated brass jump rings (which we'll call the "small rings") to create the double-spiral chain for the pendant. Close two of these rings and open the other 76 rings **(Chain Mail Techniques and Tips, p. 104)**. You will need an additional four small rings (all open) to join the ends of the double-spiral chain together and attach the crystal.

**2|** Pick up an open small ring, and place it through the hole in the pear-shaped crystal. Close the ring. Pick up another open small ring, and place it through the first small ring. Close the ring. Pick up a third open small ring, and place it through the second small ring. Close the ring **[A]**. Set this piece aside for now.

**3|** To start your double-spiral weave, insert a twist tie through the two closed small rings. This will form a "handle" that will help you hold and stabilize the weave. Pick up an open small ring and place it through the two closed small rings **[B]**. Close the ring. Add another open small ring beside it, following the same path, and close the ring.

**4|** Position the two sets of small rings so that they overlap to create an "eye." Make sure that the second set of rings lies on top of the previous set of rings on the upper side of the eye (and they will also lie underneath the previous set of rings on the lower side of the eye). Pick up an open small ring and pass it through the eye where the sets of rings overlap **[C]**. Close the ring. Add another open small ring beside it, following the same path, and close the ring.

## MATERIALS >>

*Necklace size: 23" (58.4cm)*

- Gold-plated brass jump rings
  - » **263** 20-gauge 4mm (.149") ID [AR 4.7]
  - » **90** 19-gauge 6mm (.215") ID [AR 6.0]
- 16mm crystal pear-shaped pendant, Swarovski [6106], ruby
- Heirloom toggle clasp, TierraCast, antique gold
- **32"** (81.3cm) of ¼" (6mm) wide satin ribbon, red
- **24"** (61cm) of polyester or nylon sewing thread, red

*Earring size: 1⅞" (48mm)*

- **164** 20-gauge 4mm (.149") ID jump rings, gold-plated brass [AR 4.7]
- **2** 16mm crystal pear-shaped pendants, Swarovski [6106], ruby
- Pair of gold-filled earring wires

## TOOLS >>

- **2** pairs of pliers (chainnose, bent chainnose, and/or flatnose)
- Twist ties
- Scissors
- Hand-sewing needle
- Straight pin
- Ruler or tape measure

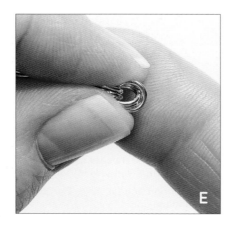

TIP This is a fairly tight weave, so if you are having difficulty getting the eye open, try inserting a toothpick through it [**D, p. 93**]. Once you have the eye open, remove the toothpick, and pinch the rings slightly between your thumb and forefinger to keep them in the correct position while you insert the next ring [**E**].

For double-spiral weave, you may find it easier to insert the rings from the back side of the weave through to the front, rather than the usual method of inserting them from the front side of the weave through to the back. Try it both ways and see which method works best for you.

**5|** Repeat step 4 until you have used 78 of the small rings. Remove the twist tie from the start of your double-spiral weave. Pick up the last open small ring and place it through the last set of rings in your double-spiral chain [**F**].

**6|** Still holding on to the last open small ring that you added at the end of your double-spiral chain, pick up the pear-shaped crystal (that has the three rings attached) with your other hand. Slip the third ring (the one farthest from the crystal) onto the open small ring so it sits to the left of the double-spiral weave [**G**].

**7|** Still holding on to the last open small ring that you added at the end of your double-spiral chain, pick up the loose end of the chain with your other hand. Bring this end of the chain up along the other side of the pear-shaped crystal [**H**].

**8|** Slip the last set of rings from the loose end of your double-spiral chain onto the open small ring, so that it sits to the left of the pear-shaped crystal [**I**]. Close the ring.

**9|** Place a twist tie through the last closed ring. You have now finished the pendant for your necklace [**J**].

## MAKE THE NECKLACE

**1|** To create the European 4-in-1 weave for the necklace, you will need 181 of the small rings: 178 of these for the necklace chain, two to attach the toggle ends, and one to attach the pendant. Close 178 of these small rings, and open three of them. You will also need 90 of the 6mm gold-plated brass jump rings (which we'll call the "large rings"). Open all of these.

**2|** Pick up an open large ring and use it to pick up two closed small rings. Close the large ring and put a twist tie through it, to use as a "handle" to hold and stabilize your weave [**K**].

**3|** Position the small rings so the side of the small rings closest to the twist tie lies on top of the large ring, and the side of the large ring farthest away from the twist tie lies on top of the small rings [**L**].

K

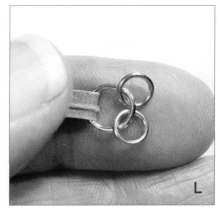

L

M

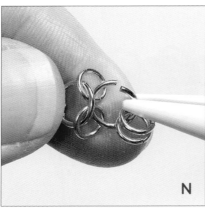

N

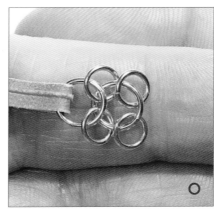

O

P

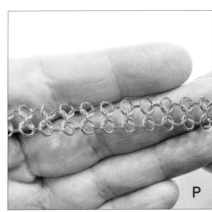

Q

R

**4|** Once you have these rings in position, pinch them slightly between your thumb and forefinger to hold them in place **[M]**.

**5|** With your other hand, pick up an open large ring and use it to pick up two closed small rings. Pass the open large ring through the small rings that you are pinching in position: through the front side of the bottom ring and up through the back side of the top ring. Make sure you don't go through the previous large ring **[N]**. Close the large ring you have just added.

**6|** Positioning the newly added rings as you did in step 3, you can see the weave configuration starting to take shape **[O]**.

**7|** Repeat steps 3–5 until you have used all but three of the small rings. Then add the last open large ring, but do not pick up and add any other rings with it. Close this large ring and put a twist tie through it **[P]**.

**8|** Cut one end of your satin ribbon at a slant, as this will make it easier to weave it through your chain. Hold your necklace chain vertically and position it so that on the side facing you, the bottom edge of each large ring sits on top of the large ring below it. Insert the beveled end of the ribbon through the first large ring at the bottom end of your chain, from the back side of the ring through to the front **[Q]**. Pull the ribbon through the ring until there is only about 1" (2.5cm) remaining **[R]**.

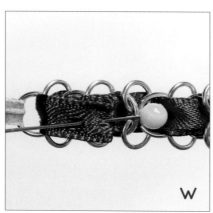

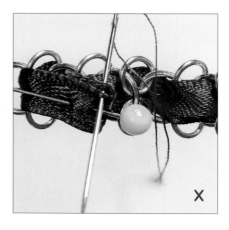

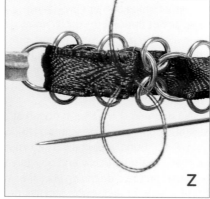

the ribbon under before you sew the edges will prevent the cut end of the ribbon from fraying.

**12|** Thread your sewing needle with 12" (30.5cm) of red thread. Align the ends of your thread evenly and knot them together.

**13|** On the upper edge of the ribbon near the folded end, push your needle through the two layers of the folded ribbon, starting from the behind the ribbon and pushing the needle towards you **[X]**. Pull the needle and thread through (this will place your thread knot between the ribbon layers, so it won't show on the front of your necklace).

Make three or four more stitches on the upper ribbon edge, close to the first stitch, going through all three layers of the ribbon for these stitches. For each stitch, push the needle through from behind the ribbon and toward you.

**9|** Weave the ribbon in and out through the large rings of your chain, weaving from the front side to the back in one ring **[S]**, then from the back side to the front in the next ring **[T]**. Make sure the 1" of ribbon that you left at the end of the weave doesn't get pulled through the chain. Gently pull the ribbon snug at each pass through the weave before moving on to the next ring. Be careful not to pull too tightly or this will cause

your chain to buckle. Check that your ribbon is pulling through straight, and not twisting, at each weave **[U]**.

**10|** At one end of your chain, fold the remaining ribbon to the back side of the necklace. Cut the remaining ribbon length to ³⁄₄" (19mm) **[V]**.

**11|** Fold the ribbon under itself ¹⁄₄" (6mm) from the end and secure it in place with a straight pin **[W]**. Folding

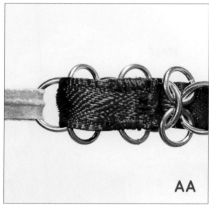

AA

BB

CC

Make sure the needle and thread don't pass through any of the jump rings.

**14|** Make a stitch across the ribbon to bring your needle out near the lower edge of the ribbon **[Y]**. Make three or four stitches on the lower ribbon edge, going through all three layers of the ribbon. For each stitch, push the needle through from behind the ribbon and towards you. Again, make sure not to catch any of the jump rings in your stitches.

**15|** Remove the straight pin. Push the needle through the folded edge of the ribbon, and pull the thread through until there is a small loop remaining. Pass your needle through this loop **[Z]**, then pull the thread tight. This is called a half-hitch knot. Tie two more half-hitch knots through the folded end of the ribbon, then cut the thread close to the last knot.

**16|** Repeat steps 10–15 to finish the ribbon at the other end of the necklace **[AA]**.

**17|** At this point, you should have three open small rings remaining. Remove the twist tie from the last ring on one end of your necklace. Pick up one of the open small rings and insert it through the loop of one piece of your toggle clasp and through the last ring where you removed the twist tie **[BB]**. Close the ring. Repeat at the

other end of the necklace to attach the other half of the toggle clasp.

**18|** Position your necklace so that the front side is facing you (i.e. the sewn ribbon ends are on the underside). You are now going to attach your pendant to the center small ring on the bottom edge of your necklace chain. The center small ring is #45 (i.e. there will be 44 small rings on either side of it), and the ribbon will be lying on top of (not underneath) this ring. Remove the twist tie from your pendant. Pick up your last remaining open small ring, pass it through the ring at the top of your pendant and through the center small ring of your necklace chain **[CC]**. Close the ring.

## MAKE THE EARRINGS

**1|** Follow steps 1–8 of "Make the pendant."

**2|** Open the bottom loop of an earring wire as you would a jump ring. Place the top ring of a pendant inside the open earring wire loop **[DD]**. Close the loop.

**3|** Repeat to make a second earring.

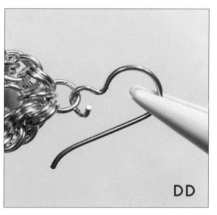

DD

## Design Variations

- Change the length of the necklace. If making the necklace chain longer, make sure both ends of the ribbon fold back to the same side, and that you have a center point to attach the pendant.

- Change the type of ribbon or cord to weave through the necklace. Try other $^3/_{16}$–$^1/_4$" (5–6mm)-wide ribbons or cords, as long as they are thin, flexible, and can be sewn at the ends. It would be interesting to see if flat leather or suede cord would work for this necklace.

# FLOWERS IN BLOOM

I love flowers and the beauty they add to our world in their amazing variety of colors, shapes, and perfumes. Flowers can also be created in chain mail using a weave made with flower links (also called Möbius links). In this bracelet and necklace set, the base of the design is a three-ring flower chain of bright silver and black-ice rings. I found that adding a black-ice ring in with the silver added contrast and depth to these flower links. Lavender flowers and sapphire channel drops "bloom" from this base, like flowers blooming in a garden.

A

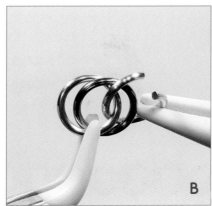

B

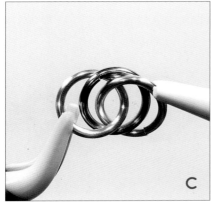

C

D

## MATERIALS >>

*Bracelet size: 7⅛" (20cm), which fits comfortably on a 7" (17.8cm) wrist*

- Anodized aluminum jump rings
  - » **36** 16-gauge ¼" (6.7mm) ID, bright silver [AR 5.5]
  - » **18** 16-gauge ¼" (6.7mm) ID, black ice [AR 5.5]
  - » **70** 18-gauge ⁵⁄₃₂" (4.1mm) ID, bright silver [AR 4.1]
  - » **51** 18-gauge ⁵⁄₃₂" (4.1mm) ID, lavender [AR 4.1]
  - » **16** 20-gauge ⅛" (3.4mm) ID, lavender [AR 4.2]
  - » **16** 20-gauge ³⁄₃₂" (2.4mm) ID, bright silver [AR 3.0]
- **16** 6mm crystal rhodium-plated round channel drops, Swarovski [57700], sapphire
- Floral toggle clasp, TierraCast, antique silver

*Necklace size: 21¾" (55.2cm)*

- Anodized aluminum jump rings
  - » **110** 16-gauge ¼" (6.7mm) ID, bright silver [AR 5.5]
  - » **55** 16-gauge ¼" (6.7mm) ID, black ice [AR 5.5]
  - » **138** 18-gauge ⁵⁄₃₂" (4.1mm) ID, bright silver [AR 4.1]
  - » **42** 18-gauge ⁵⁄₃₂" (4.1mm) ID, lavender [AR 4.1]
  - » **13** 20-gauge ⅛" (3.4mm) ID, lavender [AR 4.2]
  - » **9** 20-gauge ³⁄₃₂" (2.4mm) ID, bright silver [AR 3.0]
- **9** 6mm crystal rhodium-plated round channel drops, Swarovski [57700], sapphire
- Floral toggle clasp, TierraCast, antique silver

## TOOLS >>

- **2** pairs of pliers (chainnose, bent chainnose, and/or flatnose)
- Twist ties
- Toothpicks

## MAKE THE BRACELET

**1|** To create the base of the bracelet, you will use 36 ¼" bright silver jump rings (which we'll call the "large silver rings") and 18 ¼" black-ice jump rings to create the flower links. You will use 36 ⁵⁄₃₂" bright silver jump rings (which we'll call the "medium silver rings") to join the flower links together and attach the toggle clasp. Close 18 of the large silver rings and open 18 of them (**Chain Mail Techniques and Tips, p. 104**). Open all of the black-ice rings and all of the medium silver rings.

**2|** Pick up an open black-ice ring and use it to pick up a closed large silver ring. Position the rings so that they overlap to create an "eye." Make sure that the black-ice ring lies on top of the large silver ring on the upper side of the eye (and it will also lie underneath the large silver ring on the lower side of the eye) **[A]**. Close the ring.

**3|** Pick up an open large silver ring and place it through the eye you created with the previous two rings. Make sure this new ring lies on top of the previous rings on the upper side of the eye **[B]**. Close the ring.

**4|** You have now created a flower link. Each ring in the link should lie on top of the ring to its left on the upper side of the eye **[C]**. Move or flip the rings if necessary to get them into this position.

**5|** Set your first flower link down. Repeat steps 2–4 to create another flower link. Pick up an open medium silver ring and place it through your second flower link **[D]**.

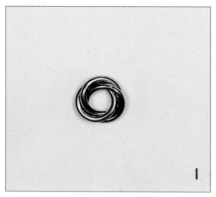

**6|** Pick up your first flower link and place it in the open medium silver ring, alongside your second flower link **[E]**. Close the ring.

**7|** Place another open medium silver ring through the two flower links, beside the first medium silver ring, and close the ring. Position the weave so that the two flower links are laying side-by-side with the medium silver rings joining them **[F]**. This is the start of your flower chain.

**8|** Continue creating new flower links and adding them to this chain until your chain is 18 flower links long **[G]**.

**9|** Pick up an open medium silver ring. Place it through the small hole in the toggle ring of your clasp and through the first flower link in your chain **[H]**.
   Repeat to attach the toggle bar of your clasp to the other end of your chain.

**10|** You will now create and attach the components to form the "blooms" of your bracelet. To create the smaller flower links, you will use 51 5/32" lavender jump rings (which we'll call the "medium lavender rings"). To attach these flower links to your bracelet base, you will use 34 of the medium silver rings. To attach the sapphire channel drops, you will use 16 1/8" lavender jump rings (which we'll call the "small lavender rings") and 16 3/32" bright silver jump rings (which we'll call the "small silver rings") Close 17 of the medium lavender rings and open 34 of them. Open all of the medium silver rings, all of the small lavender rings, and all of the small silver rings.

**11|** Using one closed medium lavender ring and two open medium lavender rings, repeat steps 2–4 to create a lavender flower link **[I]**.

**12|** Position your bracelet base with the toggle ring on the left. Pick up an open medium silver ring. Place it through the lavender flower link and through the bottom of the silver flower link immediately to the right of the toggle ring. Close the ring **[J]**.

**13|** Pick up another open medium silver ring. Place it through your lavender flower link and through the bottom of the second silver flower link in the chain. Close the ring **[K]**. Your lavender flower link should now sit between the first and second silver flower links in the chain.

**14|** Create another lavender flower link. Pick up an open medium silver ring. Place it through the lavender flower link and through the bottom of the second silver flower link in the chain. Don't cross through any of the rings of the previous lavender flower link. Close the ring **[L]**.

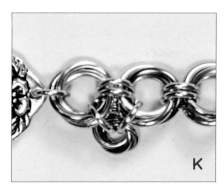

K

L

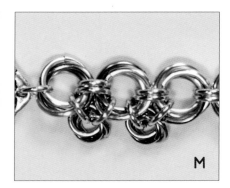

M

N

O

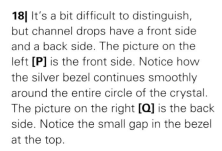

P

Q

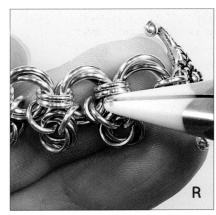

R

**15|** Pick up another open medium silver ring. Place it through the second lavender flower link and through the bottom of the third silver flower link in the chain. Close the ring **[M]**. This lavender flower link should now sit between the second and third silver flower links in the chain.

**16|** Continue creating lavender flower links and adding them to your bracelet base until you have added a total of 17 lavender flower links. You should now have a lavender flower link between every two adjacent silver flower links along the entire length of the bottom edge of your bracelet **[N]**.

**17|** Pick up an open small silver ring and place it through the loop of one of the channel drops **[O]**. Close the ring.
Repeat until you have attached small silver rings to 16 channel drops.

**18|** It's a bit difficult to distinguish, but channel drops have a front side and a back side. The picture on the left **[P]** is the front side. Notice how the silver bezel continues smoothly around the entire circle of the crystal. The picture on the right **[Q]** is the back side. Notice the small gap in the bezel at the top.

**19|** Identify the rightmost lavender flower link on the bracelet, closest to the toggle bar. Pick up an open small lavender ring and place it through the medium silver ring that is attached on the left side of the lavender flower link **[R]**.

S

T

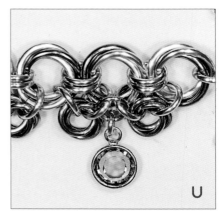

U

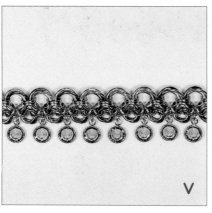

V

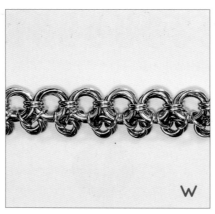

W

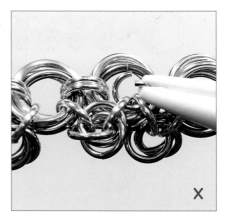

X

Y

**20|** Continue holding the open small lavender ring in this position. Pick up a channel drop. Place the small silver ring that is attached to it onto the open small lavender ring so the channel drop sits to the left of the medium silver ring that the small lavender ring has passed through. Make sure the front side of the channel drop faces towards you **[S]**.

**21|** Continue holding onto the open small lavender ring. Now place it through the medium silver ring that is attached on the right side of the next lavender flower link to the left **[T]**. Close the ring.

**22|** The channel drop should now be sitting between the last two lavender flower links on the right side of the bracelet, aligning it with the center of the second silver flower link from the right **[U]**.

**23|** Continue adding a channel drop between every two adjacent lavender

flower links, moving left along the bottom edge of the bracelet, until you have added a total of 16 channel drops **[V]**.

## MAKE THE NECKLACE

**1|** To create the necklace, you will need 110 large silver rings (55 closed and 55 open), 55 black-ice rings (all open), 138 medium silver rings (all open), 42 medium lavender rings (14 closed and 28 open), 13 small lavender rings (all open), and nine small silver rings (all open).

**2|** Follow steps 2–9 from the bracelet instructions to create a necklace base with 55 silver flower links and attach your toggle clasp at the ends.

**3|** Position your necklace with the toggle ring on the left. As in step 11 of the bracelet instructions, create a lavender flower link. Follow steps 12 and 13 of the bracelet instructions to attach this lavender flower link to the bottom edge of your necklace base so

that it sits between the 21st and 22nd silver flower links from the left. Continue creating lavender flower links and adding them to your necklace base, moving from left to right, until you have added a total of 14 lavender flower links **[W]**.

**4|** Pick up an open small lavender ring and follow steps 19–21 of the bracelet instructions to use the ring to link together the first and second lavender flower links from the right. Do not add

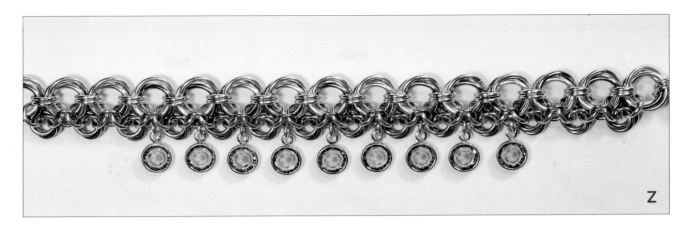

a channel drop onto this small lavender ring [X]. Repeat to use a small lavender ring to link together the second and third lavender flower links from the right, again without adding a channel drop.

5| Follow step 17 of the bracelet instructions to attach small silver rings to nine channel drops. Pick up an open small lavender ring and follow steps 19–21 of the bracelet instructions to use the ring to link together the third and fourth lavender flower links from the right. This time, add a channel drop to the small lavender ring [Y].

6| Continue adding a small lavender ring with a channel drop between every two adjacent lavender flower links, moving left along the bottom edge of the necklace until you have added a total of nine channel drops. For the last two adjacent sets of lavender flower links, link them together with small lavender rings without a channel drop, just as you did when you started at the first lavender flower links on the right side [Z].

## Design Variations

- Use Swarovski crystal navettes or oval channel drops in place of round channel drops.

- Change the type of drop: for example, use 6mm round gemstone beads (on a headpin with a wrapped loop) instead of channel drops.

## HOLDING YOUR PLIERS

Hold your pliers deep within the palm of your hand, rather than with the tips of your fingers and thumb [A]. One side of the pliers handle should be seated against the fleshy pad at the base of your thumb, with the other side of the handle sitting between the first and second joints of your other fingers. This gives you better control of the pliers and prevents hand fatigue [B, C].

## HOLDING YOUR JUMP RINGS

Before opening or closing a jump ring, it's important to position your pliers so you have a good grip on the ring. By "good grip," I don't mean squeezing hard with the pliers. It's actually best to hold the rings just tight enough to keep them from slipping out of your grasp. What I mean by "good grip" is that you have positioned your pliers on the ring to give you the best leverage to smoothly and evenly open/close the ring. Gripping the ring with only the tips of the pliers won't give you the leverage you need [D].

Position your pliers to the left and to the right of the gap in the ring, so that the plier tips are near the gap (but not covering it) and a good portion of the ring is held within the plier jaws [E]. I hold chainnose pliers in my right hand and bentnose pliers in my left

hand (these are my preferred tools). Depending on which pliers you prefer, your grip could look a bit different, but the principles of plier tips near the gap and having a good portion of the ring within the pliers is the same.

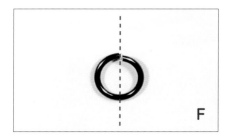

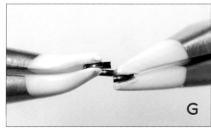

## OPENING JUMP RINGS

To open the jump ring, imagine there is an axis line running through the center of the ring, directly through the gap, as shown by the dotted line in the picture **[F]**. You want to open your ring along this axis. To do this, position your pliers correctly on the ring, then rotate your hands so that the left side of the ring moves away from you along this axis and the right side moves toward you along this axis **[G]**. Try to keep a smooth, even movement and apply equal pressure with both hands.

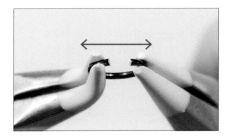

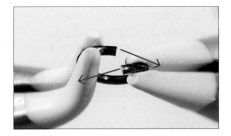

**Do not** pull the ring open to the left and the right, rather than back and forward.

**Do not** open the ring lopsided (namely, not opening it along the axis).

**Do not** let the ends of the rings twist; keep them facing directly left and right.

## HOW WIDE TO OPEN JUMP RINGS

How wide you will need to open your jump rings depends on what you need to do with them. Most of the time, opening the ring so that the gap is about three times the width of the wire is fine **[H]**.

You will need to open the ring wider if you will be putting several other rings inside it (for example when joining flower links, such as in the "Timeless Triskele" earrings, p. 17) or when you need to pass the ring through a larger component (such as through the Infinity links in the "Ad Infinitum" bracelet, p. 38).

On the other hand, a narrower opening works better when you need to add a second ring, following the same path, beside a ring that passes through several other rings. An example of this is the end sections of the "Queen of the Nile" bracelet, p. 72.

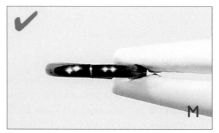

**From the side, both rings look closed [J, L]. However, you can see from the top-down view that the first ring [K] is still slightly open, while the second ring [M] is properly closed.**

## CLOSING JUMP RINGS

It's important to close your jump rings properly to get a tight, even join at the ends. This will make your jewelry look well-made and professional. Uneven joins can make your pieces look ragged and unfinished.

The method for closing jump rings is simply the reverse process of opening them, with one difference. Position your pliers correctly on the opened ring, then rotate your hands so that the left side of the ring moves toward you along the axis and the right side moves away from you along the axis. This will bring the ends of the jump ring toward each other. The difference is that you also need to push inward slightly as the ends get close to each other. Keep going with the hand rotation until the ends meet each other in the center, then go a bit farther so that they pass each other and also overlap a bit (from pushing inward) [I].

Stop at this point and let go of the ring with one hand. The ends of the ring will spring back toward the center. Check the ring by looking at it from both the side and from the top to see if the ends are joined together evenly and there is no gap between them. If you only check the ring from one angle, you might miss the fact that it's not quite joined evenly. In this example [J], the ring looks pretty well-closed from the side view, but in the top-down view [K], you can see that it actually is not.

If the ends are not quite aligned with each other, then take hold of the ring again with both pliers in correct position. Move the ends back and forth a bit more, staying in line with the axis and pushing inward slightly. Check the alignment of the ring again after a few moves. Continue these steps until the ends are joined evenly [L, M].

Patience and practice are two of the most important elements in learning to open and close jump rings to get a tight join. The movements may feel awkward at first, and you're likely to have some moments of frustration when those darned ring ends just don't seem to want to cooperate with you. Stick with it and you'll find that it becomes easier and feels more natural as you get used to holding your pliers and handling your rings.

When closing jump rings, you'll notice the amount they spring back is different, depending on the metal the ring is made of and the gauge of the wire. Jump rings made of softer metals and thinner wire (such as 22-gauge copper) will have less springback than those made with harder metals and thicker wire (such as 16-gauge anodized aluminum). (Springback is the tendency of metal to return to its original shape after it has been bent.) For any type of jump ring, opening and closing the ring causes it to become stiffer at the point where the metal is bending, which is called "work-hardening." Opening and closing a ring too many times will cause the metal to become brittle and then break.

## WHEN TO OPEN/CLOSE YOUR JUMP RINGS

When should you open (and close) your rings in preparation for a project? All at the beginning, in small batches, or one-at-a-time as needed? This is really a matter of personal preference, but you will want to consider exactly how many rings need to be opened (or closed) in total. If it's a simple earring project and requires only a few rings to be prepared, you might want to do it all at the beginning. However, if you need to prepare a large amount of rings, you might want to do this in batches. One reason is that (at least for me) this is the "boring but necessary"

part of chain mail, and I find it's a nice break to switch back and forth from preparing to mailling.

A more significant reason is that repeated motions over long periods of time are hard on your body and can result in conditions such as repetitive strain injury. When mailling, it's important to take breaks—change the tasks you're working on, get up and walk around, and stretch your muscles. This will help keep you healthy and enjoying the techniques for a long time.

## COUNTING JUMP RINGS

When you're preparing batches of jump rings or when you've started weaving a chain, it can be a challenge to keep track of the count of your jump rings. What I've found that works well for me is to lay out my rings on my chain mail mat in groupings that allow me to count them easily at a glance.

I most often lay them out in groupings of 10, in a 3-2-3-2 pattern (as shown below) that is easy to count with a quick look. When I'm a few rings along weaving a chain, I can look at my mat and know how many rings I've used. For example, if I've laid out 50 opened and 30 closed rings in this batch, and there's now 30 opened and 18 closed rings left on my mat, then I know I've used 20 opened and 12 closed rings so far in my weave. I find it helpful to keep a notepad and pen beside my mat to write down how many rings I've prepared in a batch, and any other items I want to keep track of.

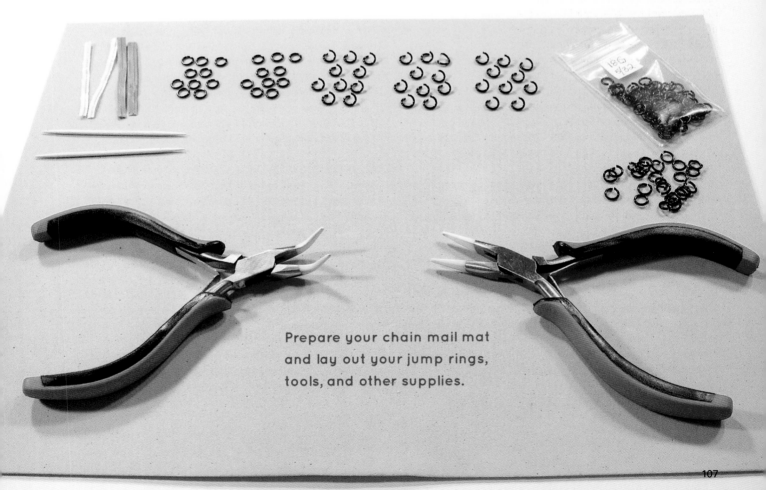

Prepare your chain mail mat and lay out your jump rings, tools, and other supplies.

## ABOUT THE ACRONYMS

ID/OD, AWG/SWG/WD, and AR … oh my! These are common acronyms used in chain mail, but can seem a bit mind-boggling if you're not familiar with them, so let me see if I can help you with this.

ID and OD are jump ring measurements. ID = inside diameter, which is the distance across the middle of the jump ring from one inside edge to the other. OD = outside diameter, which is the distance across the middle of the jump ring measured from the outside edges.

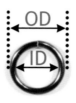

AWG and SWG are measurements of wire gauge, which is the thickness of the wire—in other words, the wire diameter (WD). AWG = American Wire Gauge (also called Brown & Sharpe); SWG = Standard Wire Gauge. In comparison of the two scales, SWG wire thicknesses are larger than AWG wire thicknesses of the same gauge number. For example, SWG 16-gauge wire is 1.63mm in diameter and AWG 16-gauge wire is 1.29mm in diameter.

### TIP
All wire gauges in the projects in this book are measured in AWG.

For both AWG and SWG, the larger the gauge number is, the thinner the wire is. For example, AWG 16-gauge wire is 1.29mm in diameter and AWG 20-gauge wire is .812mm in diameter.

In chain mail, AR = Aspect Ratio, which is a comparison of the size of the wire to the size of the inside of the ring. It is an indicator of how many rings you can fit inside a jump ring of the same size.

**The formula for Aspect Ratio is: ID ÷ WD = AR**

Let's try out this formula for one of the jump rings used in several of the projects in this book: a 20-gauge (AWG) $^5/_{32}$" anodized aluminum jump ring. To use the formula, we need to convert all measurements to the same system. For this example, I'm going to convert to millimeters, although the formula works just as well with inches.

If you convert $^5/_{32}$" to metric, you get a measurement of 4.0mm (if you round the number to one decimal place). For this jump ring, however, the actual ID is 4.3mm. This is related to the concept of springback. To make the jump rings, the aluminum wire is wrapped around a $^5/_{32}$" mandrel. When the coils are removed from the mandrel, the springback of the metal causes them to expand slightly, which makes the ID larger.

The second number we need for the formula is the wire diameter which, for AWG 20-gauge wire, is .812mm.

So, we have: **4.3mm (ID) ÷ .812mm (WD) = 5.3 (AR)**

You may be wondering what this has to do with chain mail and why we even have to bother with it. The reason is that AR determines which chain mail weaves you can make with the jump rings and what your weave will look like.

Most chain mail weaves have a range of ARs that work well for the weave. On the lower end of the range, the weave will appear more condensed and compact, while on the upper end of the range, the weave will be looser and more open. If the AR of the rings is too low for the weave, your weave might become so tight that it will lock up and you won't be able to pass the rings through. If the AR of the rings is too high for the weave, your weave might become so floppy that it can't properly hold the pattern.

A good example of the impact of AR occurred when I was designing the Cord-ially Yours bracelet for this book. I originally did the queen's braid weave with 18-gauge $^5/_{32}$" anodized aluminum jump rings, which have an AR of 4.1. I loved the dense and substantial look of the weave, but I found that the AR was too tight to allow me to insert the 16-gauge $^1/_4$" rings (which were required to attach the leather) on the sides of the queen's braid chain. I ended up switching the queen's braid to 20-gauge $^5/_{32}$" rings, which have an AR (as shown in our formula example) of 5.3, and this worked perfectly.

For each jump ring used in this book, all of the details (ID, wire gauge, and AR) are provided for you, and are included in the list of materials for each project.

# ABOUT THE WEAVES

## JAPANESE

Japanese weave is characterized by horizontal rings (usually single or double) joined together by vertical rings (usually single or double). The vertical rings are generally smaller than the horizontal rings. If there is a significant size difference between the two, this can create a tight weave which can form quite sturdy, flat geometric shapes, such as triangles, hexagons, and others. An example can be seen in the triangle base in the "Trending Triangles" earrings, p. 13.

## EUROPEAN 4-IN-1

European 4-in-1 weave is one of the best-known chain mail weaves, as it was used to create armor for knights in medieval Europe. This is a flat weave where every ring passes through four other rings, creating a mesh-like fabric that expands and contracts in one direction of the weave, but will hold fairly firm in the other direction. It can be woven as a single row (as seen in the "Red Carpet" necklace, p. 92) or as a wider sheet that can form a base for attaching links and charms (as seen in the "Made With Love" bracelet, p. 79).

## HELM CHAIN

Helm chain is also known as parallel chain and celtic line. This weave is made with two sizes of rings, and the smaller rings must be able to fit completely inside the larger rings and still have a bit of extra room. This weave uses orbital rings (which are rings that go around other rings, but don't pass through any rings), sandwiching them between other rings to create a firm, flat chain (as seen in the "Triple Wrap-sody" bracelet, p. 43).

## FLOWER LINKS

Flower links are also called rosette links and möbius links. In this weave, every ring goes through each and every other ring. A minimum of two rings are needed to make a flower link. The maximum number of rings that can be used is determined by the AR of the rings (i.e. how many will fit inside the flower link) and also by the look you want to achieve. Flower links can

be made to spiral in either a clockwise or counter-clockwise direction (as seen in the "Timeless Triskele" earrings, p. 17).

## DOUBLE-SPIRAL

Double-spiral weave is also known as spiral 8-in-2 and rope weave. Unlike the single-spiral weave, which untwists unless both ends are secured, the double-spiral weave holds its shape. If it is woven with rings that are close to the minimum AR for this weave (which is 4.6), it produces a dense-appearing rope (as seen in the "Queen of the Nile" bracelet and earrings, p. 72).

## QUEEN'S BRAID

Queen's braid weave is also known as Inca puno and box chain. In this weave, every second set of rings is folded back, before the next set is added. This creates a four-sided chain, where the folded rings form "V" shapes which face the same direction. This weave looks best if done with rings with an AR of 4.8 and above, which gives the chain a square cross section (as seen in the "Denim Daydreams" earrings, p. 21). If done with rings with an AR below 4.8, the weave becomes rectangular, but the sides don't hold a stable shape and they will flip back and forth between being the wide or narrow side of the rectangle.

## BYZANTINE

Byzantine weave is known by many other names, including fool's dilemma, idiot's delight, and birdcage weave. It is woven similarly to queen's braid, but every third set of rings is folded back (rather than every second set), before the next set is added. This creates a very decorative chain, with "V" shapes in alternating directions (as seen in the "Charms in Harmony" bracelet, p. 26). A variation of this weave is half Byzantine, where every fourth set of rings is folded back (as seen in the "Forever Lavender" necklace, p. 49).

## Overhand Knot

Make a loop in the cord and pass the working end through it. Pull the ends to tighten the knot.

## Plain Loop

**1|** Trim the wire, eyepin, or headpin ⅜" (1cm) above the top bead. Make a right-angle bend close to the bead.

**2|** Grab the wire's tip with roundnose pliers. The tip of the wire should be flush with the pliers. Roll the wire around the jaw of the pliers to form a half-circle. Release the wire.

**3|** Reposition the pliers in the loop and continue rolling.

**4|** The finished loop should form a centered circle above the bead.

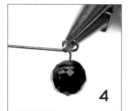

## Wrapped Loop

**1|** Make sure you have at least 1¼" (3.2cm) of wire above the bead. With the tip of your chainnose pliers, grasp the wire directly above the bead. Bend the wire (above the pliers) into a right angle.

**2|** Using roundnose pliers, position the jaws in the bend.

**3|** Bring the wire over the top jaw of the roundnose pliers.

**4|** Reposition the pliers' lower jaw snugly into the loop. Curve the wire downward around the bottom of the round-nose pliers. This is the first half of a wrapped loop.

**5|** Position the chainnose pliers' jaws across the loop.

**6|** Wrap the wire around the wire stem, covering the stem between the loop and the top bead. Trim the excess wire and press the cut end close to the wraps with chainnose pliers.

# ACKNOWLEDGMENTS

I am eternally grateful to my husband and daughter—to both of them for their critiques of my prototype designs for this book, to Cal for working with me through many long hours of process photography, and to Jessica for her diligent proofreading of my initial written drafts. But perhaps most of all, for being there and seeing me through this journey, from beginning to end. I love you guys!

Many thanks to TierraCast for providing many of the beautiful metal components I used to create the jewelry in this book. A special thanks to Kelli Taylor, who was so kind in responding to my request and in making the arrangements.

My gratitude to Swarovski for providing their fabulous crystal components for many of the jewelry pieces in this book. I would especially like to thank Kim Pennacchia, for so graciously receiving my request and organizing the delivery.

Thank you to everyone on the Kalmbach publishing and marketing teams: Lisa Schroeder, Bill Zuback, Erica Barse, Janice Zimdars, and Nanette Fox. And thank you to Dianne Wheeler for opening the door.

# ABOUT THE AUTHOR

### Sandy Haugen

Handicrafts have been an essential part of Sandy's life for as long as she can remember, starting with spool knitting as a child and designing her first original needlepoint picture for a high school art class. She has been making hand-crafted jewelry for the past ten years. In addition to her love of chain mail, she also enjoys bead weaving, bead crochet, kumihimo, and cross-stitch. She and her husband, Cal, operate StravaMax Jewelry Etc., an online store. Their daughter, Jessica, is a graphic designer and jewelry artist who contributes beautiful graphics and wirework jewelry to the family business. In Sandy's "other life," she works as a Registered Nurse. She and her family live in Kamloops, in beautiful British Columbia, Canada. Sandy can be contacted (and her jewelry, kits, and supplies can be found) at www.StravaMax.com and at www.etsy.com/shop/StravaMax.

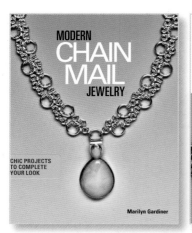

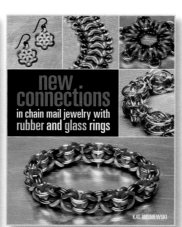
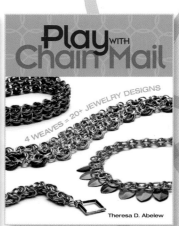